The Resurgence of Freemasonry

Also by the Author

Freemasonry: An Introduction
(Tarcher/Penguin, 2011)

The Mysteries of Freemasonry:
Essays on Masonic History, Symbolism, the Esoteric,
and the Future of Freemasonry
(The School of Freemasonry™ Books, 2017)

Masonic Education:
A Guide for Instructors and Speakers
(The School of Freemasonry™ Books,
forthcoming in Fall 2018)

The Resurgence of Freemasonry

Why Masonry Must Not Just Survive but *Thrive* — And How Masons and Their Lodges Can **Make That Happen**

Mark E. Koltko-Rivera, Ph.D.

THE SCHOOL OF FREEMASONRY™ BOOKS

an imprint of
FREE-MASONIC MEDIA
Weehawken, New Jersey, USA
2018

The Resurgence of Freemasonry: Why Masonry Must Not Just Survive but Thrive—and How Masons and Their Lodges Can Make That Happen by Mark E. Koltko-Rivera, Ph.D.

First edition, published August 2018 by The School of Freemasonry™ Books, an imprint of Free-Masonic Media, Weehawken, New Jersey, USA.

ISBN-13: 978-0-6157-8124-2   ISBN-10: 0-6157-8124-1

U.S. editions printed in the United States of America.

Front cover illustration: Pablo Twose Valls, via flickr

Back cover author photo by Katherine Finkelstein:
    katherinefinkelstein.com
www.koltkorivera.com

Copies of this book may be purchased online at:
    http://astore.amazon.com/marswri-20

Dedication

To my children, their spouses, and all their children

for all of whose sake
I hope, pray, and work so that
Freemasonry resurges
and its values suffuse the world

Table of Contents

continued

List of Figures

Preface

I want Freemasonry to thrive.

Why? I want the Craft to thrive for two reasons, one "micro" and one very "macro."

On the micro level, I have seen the power of the principles of Freemasonry to influence men, to change them, even to transform them, from basically good men into far better men. This in and of itself is a most excellent thing, for to better even a single human life is the best and most noble work that one can aspire to in one's own life.

On the macro level, however, there is an even greater urgency to ensure that Freemasonry thrives. To explain this urgency, I need to get very "big picture" — because, in a very real way, the future of the human race depends upon the values that Freemasonry promotes.

We are each seeing in our own lifetimes more real change in the conditions of human life than the human race has seen in any three prior centuries combined. The human world is no longer a collection of isolated cultures. We are witnessing the emergence, for the first time in recorded history, of a planetary human civilization. We are on the brink of humankind's emergence from infancy. And yet, this period is fraught with not just opportunity, but actual peril.

Not long ago, the technology writer and book reviewer Lev Grossman wrote this about a book by Pulitzer Prize-winning author and oncologist Siddhartha Mukherjee:

> "Three profoundly destabilizing ideas ricochet through the twentieth century," he [Mukherjee] writes, "trisecting it into three unequal parts: the atom, the byte, and the gene." These are the fundamental units of matter, information, and life, and in all three cases, as the work shifted inevitably from learning to read these primal languages to learning to write in them, explosive powers and energies were released. (Grossman, 2016, p. 56)

And so it is. As we have advanced in our knowledge of physics, information science, and genomic science, we have gained the power to create marvels—and to destroy everything that anyone has ever known, in multiple ways. What will determine whether we go in the direction of greater life, or destruction and death?

Wisdom.

Encompassing knowledge, but more than knowledge alone, wisdom reflects insight, judgment, the ability to take multiple perspectives into account, and the ability to assess and choose among potential consequences. As the renowned psychologist Robert Sternberg has explained it, wisdom involves applying intelligence, knowledge, and creativity to achieving *a common good* that balances self-interest, others' interests and welfare, and the interests of "other aspects of the context in which one lives ..., such as one's city or country or environment or even God" (Sternberg, 2003, p. 152). As he put it, "such a power [as wisdom] would seem to be of vast importance in a world that at times seems bent on destroying itself" (p. 147). This is pure truth.

We need to develop wisdom not just on a personal level, but on a societal scale. We need to raise the level of wisdom for the human race, and we need to begin this effort in our lifetime—or there could very well *be* no further lifetimes.

Freemasonry can be a powerful vehicle for developing wisdom, in such a way that not just individuals but entire societies are transformed. We have done this before. We can do this again.

By promoting such ideas as the three principal tenets of our profession, the four cardinal virtues, and the study of the liberal arts and sciences; by inculcating the lessons of the many working tools of the Mason; by leading men to ponder the lessons offered by the three great lights in Freemasonry, the three great pillars of the Lodge, and the deeper mysteries of our symbols; by focusing on the common good in the lessons of the Level and the Trowel—by all these things, Freemasonry helps to deepen men, and make them wiser. This is no small thing, especially in an age such as ours.

The popular culture that prevails in the West in our day is bent on instant gratification, hedonism, narcissism, empty fame, and superficiality. It is a popular culture whose attention flits from one shiny object to another, thereby forming minds with the attention spans of squirrels. Even when clothed in the trappings of academic degrees, startup business plans, and computer coding skills, the popular mindset of our day is focused on creating sparkly technology without considering the deeper issues of why and how such technologies might—or might not—be used for good. Answering—even forming—such questions requires wisdom. And at nurturing wisdom, Masonry excels, when it is actually implemented.

This is why I want Freemasonry not just to survive in the 21st century and beyond, but to **thrive**. I want Masonic ideals to become a stronger influence in American society, in *all* societies, and in all of the emerging global civilization, than they have ever been before. That is why I have written this book.

As I document below, if we continue on as we have over the last three generations or so, Freemasonry will *not* thrive. Let me be clear: if we continue on with business as usual, **Freemasonry is headed for virtual extinction**, a status so weak that it might as well be extinct.

And so it is that we must, each of us, change our ways—not just for the sake of the Fraternity, but for the sake of the society in which our children and our children's children will live, and even for the sake of all human civilization.

Who am I to write such a book as this?

First and foremost, I am a Freemason. I was raised a Master Mason in Winter Park Lodge No. 239 F&AM in Florida; having moved back to the Northeast of the United States, I am now also a member of Heritage Lodge No. 371 F&AM and Joshua Lodge No. 890 F&AM in New York. In addition, I am a member of appendant and invitational bodies in Florida, New York, or both, including the Scottish Rite and the York Rite. I have the honor of being the Past Grand Historian of the Grand Lodge of Free and Accepted Masons of the State of New York.

Secondly, I have written and published as a scholar of Freemasonry. My book, *Freemasonry: An Introduction* (Tarcher/Penguin, 2011) has reached a wide readership. My articles on the Craft have appeared in the *Philalethes* magazine, and in the publications of the American Lodge of Research (New York), the Florida Lodge of Research, and the Scottish Rite Research Society. (However, I note that no Masonic body or other organization has commissioned, sanctioned, or granted approval to this book.)

Finally, my writing is informed by my research and study in psychology. I hold a doctorate from the Department of Applied Psychology at New York University (Ph.D., 2000), and I have been elected a Fellow of the American Psychological Association. My research and published scholarship in psychology has resulted in awards from the Society for the Psychology of Religion and Spirituality, the Society for Humanistic Psychology, and the Society for General Psychology.

Thus, I write from the position of an active Freemason who is informed about the philosophical and historical background of the Fraternity, and whose writing is informed by research and theory in individual, social, and cultural psychology.

A note about language: I address myself here to what is known as 'mainstream' or 'regular Freemasonry,' which is a male organization. So it is that I speak about *men*, a *man*, and *his* lodge.

Another limitation in this book is that I focus on Freemasonry in the United States. Although the plan I describe here would be useful in other jurisdictions (particularly those which primarily function in the English language), I have no direct experience with Masonic lodges outside the United States. On the other hand, I have over a decade of experience as a Mason in two widely separated States in the U.S., and I am in direct (almost daily) contact with Masons in lodges across the country (and outside the U.S). I have good reason to believe that the plans I lay out here would be quite useful in United States lodges; if those in other jurisdictions find merit in these ideas, I am all the more gratified.

I am very grateful to Master, Wardens, and Trustees of Service City—Geba Lodge #1009 F&AM (New York), and to the Curator and the Trustees of The Chancellor Robert R Livingston Masonic Library of Grand Lodge (New York) for extending me opportunities to make my first two public presentations on these ideas, in the Fall of 2016.

My hope is that this book will help Freemasons to do what is needed to help our Fraternity to thrive, to grow and develop into the force it needs to be, in order to help many 'good men become better' in the 21st century and beyond, and to help guide our civilization to greatness. As brethren of a former day said:

> *Amen, amen, so mote it be,*
> *So say we all for charity.*

—Mark E. Koltko-Rivera, Ph.D., M∴M∴, 32°, K.T.

Weehawken, New Jersey, U.S.A.

August 20, 2018, in the Masonic Year of Light, 6018 A.L.

www.koltkorivera.com   mekrhub.com

The Resurgence of Freemasonry

Introduction

The world needs Masonic values, more than ever before. A world torn by ethnic, sectarian, and political strife needs a brotherhood of enlightened gentlemen to show it how to tolerate differences and deal with disagreement in peaceful, rational ways. A world of godless horror and hedonism needs men who put their trust in God. A world where sheer mindless emotion moves nations needs a rational league of men who keep their passions within due bounds, who follow reason, and who apply logic.

Freemasonry could bring all of this to the world. Masonic philosophy helped bring representative democracy to Europe (and thus many of its colonies). Masonic principles helped to bring forth the United States, where several of these principles are embodied in the American Constitution. But Freemasonry in our age is much diminished from what it once was. How could Freemasonry ever recover, and help to change our world again?

This book can help *you* make Freemasonry a great force for good in the world—a greater force for good than the Craft has *ever* been before.

Yes, *you*, personally. I imagine that most readers of this book will be rank-and-file members of their local lodges— perhaps serving on a committee; probably not in the officer line, although maybe a reader here and there may serve as the Tyler, a Marshal, or one of the Stewards. (Some readers, it is true, may even be Deacons, Wardens, Masters of Lodges, or

Grand Lodge officers.) You may not think that you have much influence to change things in your lodge, let alone in the Fraternity as a whole—but you do.

This book will show you how to exercise a great deal of influence, starting in your own small corner of the world, and in your own lodge, and extending from there, over time, to the entire Fraternity, and to the world at large.

I am utterly serious about this. The ideas that I present here can help you personally, your Particular Lodge, your Masonic district, and your Grand Lodge, to build a high-quality Freemasonry that in turn can have a strong influence for good in the world—**a stronger influence than the Fraternity has *ever* had.**

Freemasons have changed the world before. We can change the world again.

Yes, I know. The received wisdom is that the "glory days" of Freemasonry are over for good.

The received wisdom is wrong.

American Freemasonry has arrived at its current state—much diminished from earlier generations, and ever shrinking—for a number of reasons:

- We have far fewer candidates for initiation than we used to have. Several factors come into play here: much of society simply does not know that we still exist; many of those who *do* know, think we are devil worshipers who conspire against humanity; many of the rest think that we are all barely living fossils, or that men must be invited to become Masons, or any of half a dozen other silly, inaccurate things about the Fraternity that keep people from petitioning for membership.

- Of the initiates we do have, quite a few drop out after a relatively short time in the Fraternity, largely because the Freemasonry that they find in the lodges just does not feed their souls. They then choose to spend their time and their membership dollars elsewhere.

- For many of those who stay in the Fraternity, Freemasonry as they encounter it in their lodges is not the transformative quest that they thought it might be—*and as it truly can be*. They don't know how to fix that, and their attachment to the Craft may decline or fade away entirely.

Each one of these factors is a problem, yes—but a problem that can be solved. Every single one of these factors can be addressed successfully. What it takes is a plan, the will, and the effort. This book provides a plan. The will and the effort must come from you.

As I will show here, there are steps that you, your lodge, your district, and your Grand Lodge can take to accomplish the following:

- Increase substantially the number of truly worthy candidates that your lodge receives.

- Make the Masonic experience in your lodge so rewarding that hardly anyone either formally demits, or informally disappears (leading to suspensions for non-payment of dues, or NPDs).

- Make Freemasonry as practiced in your lodge into a transformative experience that makes good
  men into *much* better men.

When Masons do these things and sustain them over time,
Freemasonry will be a force for much good in our families,
our communities, and even in the world at large. *Indeed, Freemasonry will become a greater force for such good than it has ever
been before.*

And this book will show you how.

This book is divided into three parts.

PART ONE: THE VISION AND THE HOPE provides a sense of
where all the effort that I recommend in this book can lead:

- Chapter 1 sketches the Masonic civilization that a
  strong Freemasonry could help to build in the
  world.

- Chapter 2 describes the Freemasonry—true to its
  nature as an initiatic institution that transforms
  men's lives—that we must nourish and build, in
  order to make the vision sketched in Chapter 1 to
  become a reality.

- Chapter 3 answers the question, why should we
  think that Freemasonry ever could grow to become the sort of institution that could affect society as I have described?

- In Chapter 4, I explain how Freemasons have a moral obligation to build the strong Masonry that I have described.

PART TWO: THE PRESENT SITUATION lays out our current circumstances:

- Chapter 5 describes briefly the situation of the world at large, demonstrating the need for the kind of muscular Freemasonry that I describe in Part One.

- In Chapter 6, I describe the current situation of the Fraternity in America, demonstrating that we need to change just to survive, let alone to thrive.

PART THREE: THE PLAN, the major part of the book, describes how we can build the Fraternity, past the point of mere survival, and well into the territory of actually thriving. In each of these chapters, I describe efforts to be made on the part of the individual Mason, his Particular Lodge, the Masonic district, and the Grand Lodge:

- Chapter 7 specifies precisely who shall bring about the work of the Masonic resurgence: the individual rank-and-file Mason, the Master of the Lodge, the District Deputy Grand Master, and the Grand Master.

- Chapter 8, "Repair the Temple," explains what we need to do to refine the experience that Masons have in the lodge.

- Chapter 9, "Build the House of Learning," explains how to conduct meaningful Masonic education in the lodge, education that has a major impact on men's lives.

- Chapter 10, "Build the Lighthouse," describes how we can tell the world about Freemasonry in a way that is both true to our commitment not to recruit, and also responsive to the fact that almost no one knows who we really are anymore.

- Chapter 11, "Repair the Western Gate," describes what we should be doing with regard to persons who have an interest in Freemasonry (before filing a petition), Petitioners, and candidates for the mysteries of Freemasonry.

- Chapter 12, "Build the Guard Towers," lays out the efforts we should be making to defend Freemasonry against the more delusional of its detractors—a group who can truly say, "we are legion."

We *can* do this. For the sake, not only of our Fraternity, but of our society as a whole, even for the sake of the world at large, we *must* do this.

Let us begin.

PART ONE

THE VISION AND THE HOPE

1

The Masonic Civilization That Could Be

The late author Stephen R. Covey noted that one habit of highly effective people is to "begin with the end in mind":

> To begin with the end in mind means to start with a clear understanding of your destination. It means to know where you're going so that you better understand where you are now and so that the steps you take are always in the right direction. (Covey, 1989/1990, p. 98)

So it is that in this chapter, I consider what our society might look like if it were more thoroughly imbued with Masonic principles. My hope is that, through pondering this vision, the reader might be motivated—even inspired—to pay closer attention to the chapters that follow, and take the actions needed to help build his Lodge and his Craft, thereby building himself, his family, his community, his society, and even his very civilization, on a more firm foundation.

A "Masonic Civilization" of the Past and Present

Many years ago, almost a decade before my own initiation as a Freemason, I came upon an issue of *Gnosis* magazine—an issue that was focused on Freemasonry. The introductory essay in that issue, by the magazine's editor, Richard Smoley, had an intriguing title: "Masonic Civilization." He wrote:

Personally I am not a Mason. I know no more of this tradition than can be found in books. Yet from the small amount of reading I've done, I'm convinced that every spiritual seeker today owes an incalculable debt to Freemasonry. You could even say that ours is fundamentally a Masonic civilization....

... One of the most influential of the seventeenth-century speculative Masons was an Englishman named Elias Ashmole, who was initiated in 1646. Ashmole ... was also one of the founders of the Royal Society, the first modern organization for scientific investigation.... Nearly all of the Royal Society's first members were Masons....

... Freemasonry has been one of the chief sponsors of republican government [that is, representative democracy] against monarchism and of rational, scientific investigation as opposed to ecclesiastical dogma....

[Freemasons] have fought to separate secular from sacred authority, culminating in achievements like the First Amendment of our own [American] Constitution....

Given that both modern science and modern democracy have Masonic origins, it's not entirely specious to contend that ours is a Masonic civilization. (Smoley, 1997, pp. 12, 14-15; footnote omitted)

Smoley's essay focused on how today's Western societies have their democratic roots in the Freemasonry of past centuries. But the title of his essay got me to thinking about what Western societies—what Western civilization—might look like if Freemasonry were again to become strong enough to have a substantial impact at the societal level.

A Masonic Civilization in the Future

Change the people who live in a society, and of course you will change the nature of that society as a whole. One does not need to change all the people, or most of the people, or even 90% of them to make a major and meaningful change. Change a small group, change people who are or who become pillars of their communities, or thought leaders within a society, and in all likelihood much of the rest of society will follow.

This is the case with both destructive and constructive forces in nature. A landslide can start with a rolling pebble, an avalanche with the disturbance caused by a single vocal shout. And yet vast forests may have their beginnings with but a single well-placed seed.

So it is with human cultures. One man has a vision in the desert or a forest; one man nails his thoughts up in the public square and states that there he makes his stand; one man describes his ground-breaking thoughts; one man walks to the sea and picks up a single pinch of salt in an act of defiance, or marches to the statehouse for justice, or treads a path to the place of his execution, his faith unwavering—and dozens follow his way, then hundreds, then thousands, then millions. In the 21st century, most of Earth's teeming billions follow ways of life based primarily on the teachings of one or the other of no more than a dozen men of the past four millennia of human history. It takes billions to make the human world, but far fewer to lead them and enrich their lives.

Let Freemasonry be such an inspiration in the 21st century. It is a time when science and technology can give us so much, or can destroy us all; the power of faith can help to heal this world, or rend it into pieces; our differences can enrich us, or divide us. In such a time as this, let the ideals of the Sons of Light, the inheritors of the European Enlightenment, inspire the world through the example and leadership of a critical mass of Masons.

And what would that world look like?

———————

Consider first the values that a critical mass of Masons could inject into the culture at large, into the very fabric of our society, from the values taught in the three basic tenets of our profession as Freemasons, the four cardinal virtues communicated in the Middle Chamber lecture, and a few other values clearly communicated in our rituals:

- **Brotherly love**, being aware that we humans are all members of one human family, across all artificial lines of race, class, politics, and religion.

- **Relief** of the distressed, as "a duty incumbent on all men."

- **Truth-telling** as the standard for communication, while hypocrisy and deceit are to be a disgust.

- **Fortitude** in good endeavors, despite difficulty or danger. (There is a reason why some lodges are named after Arctic and Antarctic explorers.)

- **Prudence** in our behavior, regulating it by reason, and in consideration of future consequences.

- **Temperance** in our enjoyments, taking care to bridle our passions and restrain our pleasures within due bounds.

- **Justice** to all without distinction, and fairness in all our dealings with others.

- **Self-improvement** as a major focus for our efforts.

- **The union of faith and reason**, where logic, science, and faith *jointly* guide our decisions and actions.

These are only a selection of the values that we instill in the new Brother. Now imagine them instilled among leadership of the society at large: the pillars of the local community (many of the shopkeepers, owners of small businesses, heads of trade unions, local police, community board members, teachers, clergy, youth group leaders), as well as many so-called opinion makers, taste makers, and thought leaders (writers, media commentators, artists of various types), and even political leaders.

What kind of society would we have? Let us consider this in terms of individual lives, then in terms of families and communities, then in terms of society as a whole.

Personal Lives

Right now, the default setting for 'the good life' in our society involves the mindless pursuit of short-term pleasure and signs of wealth. (Think of the typical slate of television commercials shown during the Super Bowl.)

By contrast, in a more Masonic civilization, a major focus of life would be self-improvement: spiritual, moral, intellectual, and emotional development. There would be a greater focus on improving physical health as a foundation for all human happiness.

More people would participate in sports, not just watch them. More people would learn about science, not just watch television shows about forensic scientists and nerdy grad students. More people would study their Volumes of Sacred Law directly, not just watch shows based on them. More people would treat others like equals, and live lives of what amounts to 'everyday holiness,' rather than just watch motion pictures about people with such lives.

Families and Communities

Right now, there are huge stresses on marriages and families. There are a variety of reasons for this stress: economic distress in the home; poor financial management; a growing trend towards infidelity; addictions galore.

By contrast, in a more Masonic civilization, more men would learn about (and model to their families) being prudent in their financial affairs, bridling their passions, being temperate in their habits, and showing 'brotherly love' and concern *at home.*

One of the greatest potential contributions of Masonic light to family life is the concept that differences of opinion are to be resolved with reason and logic, rather than the imposition of authority or brute force. The lessons of the Trowel are never more important to remember than at home. And if harmony is a major support of all institutions (as Masons hear so frequently), then this is most true of all within the often-fragile boundaries of the family.

Major growth in the Craft would result in more families being warmed by Masonic light. And the goodness created in our families by this Masonic light would spread outwards to our communities, and beyond.

Society and its Sense of Mission

Would the injection of Masonic ideals and principles on a larger scale into society cure all of society's problems? Of course not; even penicillin was not a magic bullet for all ills. But such an injection would take a huge bite out of American society's problems, and improve the lives of millions.

Let me put it this way. Truly has it been said that 'the personal is political,' and one way that this principle manifests is in the way that personal failings have affected the national political process.

In my adult life, I have seen one American President forced to resign because of illegal activities, another President considered for impeachment because of his unbridled passions, a former Speaker of the U.S. House of Representatives ruined by *his* unbridled passions, a sitting U.S. Congressman and a state Governor forced to resign their offices for *their* unbridled passions, and so on and so on. I have seen mayors of major cities ruined by their intemperance. I have seen the world economy nearly melted to slag by a combination of massive financial mismanagement and monumental greed. In other words, at this point, *any improvement would be welcome!*

One of the greatest contributions that Masonic ideals and principles could make to society is in terms of a sense of mission. Right now, American society is geared largely to the creation of wealth, and that mostly for the benefit of only a few. We seem to have little or no sense of societal 'mission,' such as the one we had during the settlement of the American West, the struggles of the First and Second World Wars, or the heyday of the Mercury, Gemini, and Apollo space programs. What is our society *for*, anyway? At this point, for many in American society, the answer is, to say the least, of rather limited scope: "I'm just in it for the money."

By contrast, in a more Masonic civilization, society might gain a much more expansive sense of mission: a mission to discover and explore the mysteries of Nature, to build up wisdom and strength, and to create beauty. This society could extend and improve life for all; this is the society that could take humanity out of our cradle on Earth. and out into the galaxy.

Masons were pivotal in creating Western science in the first place, through founding the Royal Society in England — the first society in the world for the promotion of rigorous, systematic scientific research — and by focusing in our ritual on the importance of reason, logic, and evidence as keys to understanding Nature. Masonic principles can be pivotal in bringing our entire society — human civilization, really — to the next level of our development, as it were.

This is the vision of Masonic Civilization that I hope will inspire the reader to engage the challenging task of building up our Fraternity—a task that begins with each Mason building up his own Particular Lodge.

In much of the remainder of this book, I will discuss the details of *how* to build the Lodge and thus the Craft. But first, I must address some important questions:

- Just what kind of Freemasonry is it that we should try to build up, in the first place?

- What would a resurgent Freemasonry look like, in terms of membership? Is such a Resurgence even possible?

- Is it really our business to take it upon ourselves to increase the membership of the Craft?

These questions are the heart of the remaining three chapters of Part One.

2

The Freemasonry That We Could Build

We want the Freemasonry that resurges to be a Masonry more devoted to its historic mission as an initiatic society that seeks to help men transform themselves. As I have written elsewhere:

> Freemasonry is a fraternity that uses ceremonies of initiation to teach symbolic lessons about philosophy, morality, and character. It is a social fellowship, a place for ritual and symbolism, and a vehicle to assist in spiritual growth. (Koltko-Rivera, 2011, p. 16)

This is a straightforward, compact definition. However, this definition comes with some serious consequences:

> If a Masonic meeting is *not* focused on these purposes—if it is not primarily about teaching or elucidating lessons about philosophy, morality, and character, building fellowship, or otherwise assisting in personal and spiritual growth—*then it has no real Masonic purpose at all.*

Yes, there will be a celebration of fraternal ties in our resurgent Freemasonry, with the Table Lodge and the Festive Board being observed more than at any time since, perhaps, the early 19th century. But this shall be no Fish-Fry Freemasonry, no program focusing on a fellowship of "euchre nights, pancake breakfasts, and bean suppers" (Knights of the North, 2006, p. 1).

Resurgent Freemasonry should have its focus firmly on the traditional concerns of the Fraternity: spiritual, moral, and intellectual growth and development, as well as fellowship.

- By **spiritual development**, I mean the Fraternity focuses upon the deepening of a Mason's relationship with the Supreme Being, and the growth of a sense of personal mission in service to humanity.

- By **moral development**, I mean the Craft helps build within the Mason a stronger commitment to the Masonic ideals of religious and political toleration; equality across lines of social class; the primacy of brotherly love, relief, and truth-telling; the four cardinal virtues and the three theological virtues—all in one's personal, business, and public affairs.

- By **intellectual growth**, I mean that resurgent Masonry instills in each Mason a focus on lifelong learning regarding the exploration of Nature and the universe, both in the outer world, and in the inner world. Intellectual growth also includes a greater commitment to, and a better understanding of, the application of reason and rationality to the issues one encounters in life and society.

- By **fellowship**, I mean the promotion of opportunities to form real friendships rather than superficial acquaintance.

This would not be a Freemasonry of empty ritualism or superficial back-slapping. It would not be a charity or service club, overlaid with ritual. It would be a true *initiatic society*, a group of men devoted to changing themselves. Such a Freemasonry would inevitably change the men who are members of it, and through them it would change the society in which they live.

What would this all look like in practical terms? I describe the nuts and bolts of creating this kind of Resurgent Freemasonry in Part Three of this book. However, at this point, let us look ahead to the outcome of these efforts, from the point of view of some members of a hypothetical Particular Lodge and Grand Lodge.

Resurgent Masonry in the Local/Particular Lodge

The brethren arrive early for the Stated Communication at Solomon's Lodge #987. It is a little on the loud side, even boisterous, as the lodge brothers greet one another like the true Brothers and friends that they are. Several knots of brethren here and there discuss the fine time they had visiting in one another's homes recently, an informal dinner accompanied by their spouses or girlfriends at this home, a televised game watched there, a friendly cutthroat game of Monopoly played somewhere else. Plans are made for more such gatherings, including a visit to a local shooting range, some informal basketball and touch football, and a movie trip or two. There would be bowling, and a round of 'Settlers of Catan.' Several brethren who had not taken part in earlier activities are invited to these future ones. None of these were 'official' Lodge activities; they were just the natural outcome of men enjoying each other's company.

Surveying the scene, the Master of the Lodge takes this all in with a smile. Several brethren ask him who is delivering the Masonic Education that evening, and the Worshipful Master is happy to report that Brother Marshal will be speaking on the symbolism of an aspect of the Third Degree ritual.

At 7:30 p.m. precisely, the gavel drops, the Lodge is called to order, and the centuries-old rituals of opening the Lodge are observed with precision and dignity. Yes, Brother Junior Deacon drops a phrase as he describes his duties—yet again, although a different phrase than the one he dropped last time—but the brethren assembled take it in stride with good nature, knowing that Brother Junior Deacon is an anxious sort, and the Senior Warden will have a friendly word with him later.

The business portion of the meeting is relatively brief, since things like the payment of the phone and utility bills were preapproved when the budget was discussed last year. There are reports from two investigations committees, an announcement of the rehearsal for the upcoming Fellow Craft Degree, a report from the committee in charge of next month's Masonic Open House, and a ballot that was returned clear. (Reports from investigation committees, and balloting, were a feature of every Stated Communication.)

After the reports and balloting are done, the next 25 minutes are spent in a session of Masonic Education. Brother Marshal has been taking the brethren through elements of Masonic ritual initiation for several months now, and his presentation tonight is excellent: well-structured and well-delivered, with a special focus of how Masons can "live out" the meaning of this symbolism in their personal lives in their families, at work and school, in their communities, and in the lodge itself.

The 25 minutes goes by quickly. Brother Marshal uses different techniques in his presentation, including interactive give-and-take with the assembled brethren: "How might the message of this symbolism play out in your lives at home?", and so forth. Brother Marshal also fields questions and encourages discussion among the brethren within the Masonic education period.

(Brother Junior Deacon makes a mental note to find out the time of the next meeting of the Lodge's Masonic Study Group, which he hears will be discussing this particular symbolism in more detail at their next meeting.)

After Lodge has been closed, the brothers meet for some light refection at a well-attended Collation; there is much discussion about life, families, work, hobbies, the Masonic Education just experienced, and plans. (A trip to an archery range is planned at one table.)

The Worshipful Master and his Wardens have noted the presence of some members they have not seen in a while, and they each have a word of welcome with these brethren privately during Collation. The Master and Wardens also note the absence of some members they usually see, and these officers arrange among themselves to make sure each of these absent brethren are called to see whether some personal care, assistance, or simple fellowship might be in order.

When the official Collation is complete, a group of brethren who do not mind the hour regroup at a local 24-hour family restaurant, where they take over the 'corner-pocket' banquette and pester the tired wait-staff for ever more blueberry pancakes as they discussed Kabbalah, tattoos, alchemy, and romance—not necessarily in that order—past midnight.

Resurgent Freemasonry in the Grand Lodge

The Grand Master has two conference calls to make each month. One is with the rest of the Elected Grand Line Officers, as they discussed Grand Lodge policies and programs. This helped not only to move the Grand Lodge along, but to provide more continuity of leadership within the Grand Lodge, as these brethren typically would be involved in these calls for several years as they progressed through the line, before reaching the Grand East.

The second conference call involves the Grand Master, Deputy Grand Master, Grand Wardens, and all of the District Deputy Grand Masters. This is how Grand Lodge's policies are promulgated, and how its programs are promoted and managed.

The Grand Master thanks heaven for Skype.

Of major concern to the Grand Master are two matters: Masonic education and Masonic reputation. These two matters are brought up in both of his conference calls every single month, regardless of whatever other business might also be discussed (such as the Masonic Home).

In terms of Masonic education, the Grand Master makes it clear that, on their official visits to Districts and Lodges, members of the Grand Line should emphasize that 20 to 30 minutes of high-quality Masonic education should be a priority in every Stated Communication; Recommendations should be made about what topics should be considered for discussion at such times. *We've really had enough about Masonic athletes,* he has said, stating that what matters is the Masonic symbolism and philosophy that make a difference in people's lives.

Part of the Grand Lodge's focus on Masonic education involves training Masons in how to plan and teach such sessions at their lodges. So it is that the Deputy Grand Master and Senior Grand Warden together plan an annual Masonic Education Day at Grand Lodge, to which each Particular Lodge is required to send at least two of its members. At Masonic Education Day, master teachers from around the jurisdiction give instruction in planning and teaching in the lodge. The capstone of the event is a session of Masonic education taught by the Grand Master himself (who has been coached in preparing and delivering this lesson by some of these same master teachers).

The Grand Master also asks his DDGM's to report on the status of Masonic education in their districts. The goal here is for *every* lodge to present 20 to 30 minutes of Masonic education at *every* Stated Communication, except when degree ceremonies are being held. The Grand Master makes it clear that this was not just an aspirational goal, but a goal that he expected to be met.

In terms of Masonic reputation, the Grand Master wants every adult in his grand jurisdiction—not just the Masons, but *every* adult—to know four things about Freemasonry:

1. Freemasonry exists today as a vibrant, living organization and tradition.

2. Masonry has nothing to do with devil worship or conspiracies to rule the world or country.

3. Freemasonry *is* concerned with making good men into better men, better in their family lives, at work and school, and in their communities.

4. There are straightforward procedures whereby any man may investigate Freemasonry for possible membership.

To get this message to the public, the Grand Master wants every lodge to hold and publicize an annual Masonic Open House. He has his DDGMs see to this, and he has the Senior Grand Warden (with the assistance of the Junior Grand Warden) plan the annual Masonic Day at Grand Lodge (essentially, the Grand Lodge Masonic Open House), to which are invited members of major print and broadcast media within the Jurisdiction.

Of course, with all this activity, there was another responsibility that the Grand Master had to attend to, almost every month.

Because there were always new lodges to charter.

Responses to Some Objections

No doubt there are some who feel that the vision I have laid out above for the Fraternity either can or should *never* be implemented, because of certain factors operating within American Freemasonry today. I respond to several of these objections below.

"You are proposing changes to Freemasonry!"

It seems to be a knee-jerk reaction on the part of some brethren to lay the charge of "proposing changes to Masonry!"

at the foot of anyone who proposes a change from the status quo. So it is that some will say that within this vision of Masonry Resurgent I am proposing fundamental changes to Freemasonry, something that is strictly forbidden by our ritual, and by many statements of the ancient Landmarks of our order. Nothing could be further from the truth.

All one has to do is consider the actual wording of any one of the three degrees of initiation in the Blue Lodge. It will be absolutely clear from such a study that Freemasonry is indeed about personal transformation along spiritual, intellectual, emotional, and moral (behavioral) lines.

No, I am not proposing changes within Freemasonry. I am sure that I am proposing changes in the way that some lodges (and even Grand Lodges) *function*. What I am proposing, essentially, is that we actually *practice* Freemasonry. For some lodges, yes, this will be a change—but it should be a welcome one.

"What is the great big deal here?"

Other brethren will make precisely the opposite objection to the one I have just mentioned. They will say that nothing I have proposed so far is all that different. Masonic education? Sure, we do that, in some lodges, or every now and then. Masonic open houses? We hold those, too—again, in some lodges, every now and then.

This objection is a serious understatement of just what it is that I am proposing here. I am not just saying that lodges should hold Masonic education. I am saying that **quality, substantial Masonic education should be the very heart of each and every Stated Communication in every Particular Lodge**.

Beyond that, I am saying that **training Masons in every Particular Lodge to deliver quality education should be one of the central functions of every Grand Lodge.** I give more detailed descriptions of how Masonic education should be conducted in Chapter 9.

How about Masonic reputation, as burnished in Masonic Open Houses? I am not just saying that lodges should have Open Houses. I am saying that *every* **lodge, including Grand Lodge itself, should hold carefully prepared and coordinated Open Houses across the Jurisdiction**. I give detailed descriptions of what should go into these Open Houses in Chapter 10.

Either regarding Masonic education or Masonic reputation activities, comparing the status quo to what I am proposing is like comparing the performance of the second-hand station wagon that I learned to drive on to the cars driven by last year's winners at the 24 Hours of Le Mans, the Dakar Rally, the Monaco Grand Prix, and the Indianapolis 500. In all cases: "it's just not in the same league."

"You are proposing that Masonry become political!"

Some will take my comments about increasing the Masonic effect on society as implying that Masonry should become more politically involved. This is not true. I am not proposing that in the slightest degree.

What I am proposing is far more important and powerful.

I am proposing that resurgent Freemasonry inspire individual Masons to act out their Masonic values in the world at large, in every aspect of their lives. Several million American Masons acting out Masonic values in their homes, their communities, their work lives—this would change American society in a completely organic way.

This is not about favoring the program of any political parties over others. One would hope that by favoring the primacy of reason, logic, and evidence, Masons would help *all* political parties to act more rationally. One would hope that by instilling an ethic of rigorous honesty in Masons of all political stripes, Masons would help instill rigorous honesty in *all* politicians. This is win-win all around.

"But this makes it sound like Masons are trying to take over the world!"

I have had people tell me personally that they are concerned that my vision of Masonic influence in the world would fan the flames of the anti-Masonic myth that Masons are trying to rule the world.

Only people who are already inclined to believe such idiocy would take what I am saying to mean that the Masons are plotting world domination. I am proposing a revolution of the soul, the heart, the mind—not some cheap conspiracy of Hollywood vintage. In a sense, I am proposing something much more important than mere world domination. I am proposing that Freemasonry be applied as it was intended: to help men transform themselves from the insight out. Anything less is a failure of the imagination.[1]

---

[1]   I make these points in much more detail in my (ironically titled) essay, "Freemasonry and World Domination: Simple Steps to Ruling the World," the final chapter of my book, *The Mysteries of Freemasonry* (Koltko-Rivera, 2017).

"Everyone likes the way things are operating now."

Another potential objection is that the typical Mason is satisfied enough with the status quo, the way things operate now. This is completely false. The large number of members who either demit (resign) from their lodges, or are expelled for non-payment of dues (NPD), demonstrates more than anything else could that a substantial number of Masons are not at all satisfied with the status quo.

John Belton, P∴M∴ surveyed almost a century's worth of Masonic membership data from the United States, Canada, Australia, and England. He reported that in these jurisdictions, not only is the average membership time (until demit or NPD, not counting deaths) is short, but is becoming shorter. As of the first half of the 1990s, the average membership time is actually **under five years**, down from about twenty years in the later 1940s, and ten years in the later 1970s (Belton, 2001, p. 19, Figure 7). He concluded, "the main cause of smaller lodges is that those who do become members stay for a much shorter period of time" (p. 18). As he put it, "the facts are clear—we have fewer new members, and **our ability to retain their interest has decreased**" (p. 18, emphasis added).

It is not that "everyone is satisfied with how things are." What has happened is that legions of Masons who were *dis*satisfied have left the Fraternity altogether. After rigorous research, Belton estimated the ten-year attrition rate at "around 50%" (p. 29).

"Today's American lodge is not that interested in this vision."

Let me issue a challenge to anyone who makes this claim. Conduct an anonymous survey, by postal mail, of the members of your lodge—every member, including those whom you have not seen in years; include a stamped return envelope. Ask the brothers at least these questions:

1. How often do you attend lodge during a given season (say, September through June or July)?

2. Would you like Stated Communications to include a 20- to 30-minute period of Masonic education, focused on Masonic symbolism and philosophy?

3. If every Stated Communication had such Masonic education, how often would you attend lodge during a given season?

Conduct that survey, report the data to me, and then tell me if that claim is still valid. Based on my own research and anecdotal experience, I am confident that you will find that your lodge brothers are very interested in this vision.

3

Why Masonry Could Resurge

Could Freemasonry indeed resurge—not just survive, but thrive, and grow to a number of Masons greater than any previous peaks in membership? If so, just how many Masons would that involve? And why should we think this is even possible, in the reality of today's world? These are the questions upon which this chapter focuses.

Are Our Best Days Behind Us?

We have heard a lot, for years, about how the circumstances that led to the huge number of members in the Fraternity in the middle of the 20th century were anomalous, particular to a specific moment in history, never to be repeated. For example, we hear this from an English brother, Daniel J. West, in a recently published book: "The golden years of Freemasonry have passed with the departure of a world never likely to return in the lifetime of anyone who might read this book" (West, quoted in Tresner, 2016, p. 27).

On this side of the Pond, some American brethren whose work I otherwise greatly admire had this to say: "The huge numbers in the [19]40's and 50's and 60's are gone forever, a statistical aberration that will never happen again" (Knights of the North, 2006, p. 1). This certainly seems to be the received wisdom.

Bosh.

I call bosh on that entire way of thinking.

Yes, it is true that huge numbers of Masons entered the American Fraternity during the period 1942 through 1959. Yes, it is true that some of this was due to the unique circumstances of the Second World War and its aftermath. And, yes, it is unlikely that this particular set of circumstances shall ever be repeated, certainly in the lifetimes of anyone reading *this* book, either.

But none of that matters in the slightest.

The fact is, as some doors have closed for Freemasonry, others have opened. If Freemasons with vision and determination take advantage of our current circumstances, our Fraternity can grow stronger than ever.

Today[2], we have our own special circumstances and opportunities. Let us consider some of these circumstances, and how they open up opportunities for the Fraternity: (1) population growth in the United States, (2) the availability of the Internet, (3) certain aspects of popular culture, and (4) the current vacuum in moral direction. Then, let us consider what the actual membership strength of a vibrant Fraternity actually is.

1. Population Growth in the United States

As of this writing in mid-2018, the population of the United States is estimated to be 327.76 million (United States Cen-

---

[2] By "today," I mean the later 2010s through the 2020s, the decade or so following the publication of this book.

sus Bureau, 2018b). This population is 85% larger than it was on July 1, 1959, when U.S. population was estimated to be 177.1 million (U.S. Dept. of Health, Education, and Welfare, 1959). I chose 1959 as the reference point, because that is the year in which American Freemasonry reached its highest membership peak to date, at 4.1 million Masons (Masonic Service Association of North America [MSANA], n.d.).

Thus, the potential pool of candidates is much, much larger in the late 2010s than it was in 1959—*by over 48 million men* (when sex and age are taken into account; see Appendix A). This alone is an important factor in making the resurgence of Freemasonry possible.

2. The Internet

The nigh-universal availability of the Internet, cheap web hosting, and website development aids means that almost any group can have an attractive multi-page website online to tell its story to the world, within an afternoon. And by "the world," I mean that portion of the Planet Earth and low orbit that has an Internet connection. Your own or your lodge's website—as well as your YouTube or Vimeo channel, or your podcast—can reach the International Space Station; it can certainly reach virtually everyone in your vicinity who has questions about Freemasonry.

3. Popular Culture

Popular culture is bringing Freemasonry into the public consciousness again. It is not only about *The Da Vinci Code* or *National Treasure*, both of which are long receded in the rear view mirror by now. There are some novelists (such as Brad Melzer, Alan Moore, and James Rollins), and events in broadcast television (such as the series *Sleepy Hollow*) and cable television (*Lodge 49*, even *Ancient Aliens*) that have put Masonry before the eyes of the public in recent years. Yes, the version of Masonry portrayed in these productions is distorted, often quite severely. But it is *something*.

Freemasonry pretty much never appeared in popular culture during my childhood or afterward, well into my forties, and I have to think that this contributed to the 57% decline in American Masonic membership between 1956 and 2002, the year before the publication of Dan Brown's *The Da Vinci Code* (see Appendix A).

4. A Vacuum in Moral Direction

It is clear that organized religion holds far less sway on the rising generation than it did on their parents and grandparents. The nature of this change, and the reasons for it, are important to understand—because, as unfortunate as these trends are, they do open opportunities for the Fraternity.

In 1972, only 11% of American adults said that they never attended religious services; among young adults, aged 18-29 years, that figure was still only 14%. In 2014, well over twice the proportion of all American adults—26%—said that they never attended religious services; among young adults, that figure expanded to 33%. Thus, fully one-third of today's American young adults never attend religious services at all (Twenge et al., 2016, pp. 5, 7).

And yet, although one-third of American young adults are essentially without organized religion in their lives, this does not mean that they have no spiritual beliefs. One-fifth of U.S. young adults who never attend religious services nonetheless believe in an afterlife, as do 80% of all young adults (p. 7). Although 28% of today's young adults say that they are "not religious at all," only 19% say that they are "not at all spiritual" (p. 7).

It seems that many young adults have a problem specifically with regard to institutional or organized religion. Why might this be so?

Based on research conducted with nearly 1,300 Americans, 18 to 29 years old, who had a Protestant or Catholic background, David Kinnaman (2011) identified several factors that led to disaffection from organized religion. These factors include the following (the labels being mine, not necessarily his):

- **Motivation by fear.** As one research participant, "Nathan," put it, "A lot of [our upbringing] was very fear-based to get you to do something as opposed to giving you logical reasons why you should or should not do something" (p. 95).

- **Superficiality times two.** As "Tracy" put it, "It just feels like in America everyone keeps faith separate from work and life" (p. 113). At the same time that many young adults feel that their churches are shallow, Kinnaman's research found that "most young people lack a deep understanding of their faith" (p. 115), echoing detailed findings reported by Stephen Prothero (2007/2008) in his landmark book, *Religious Literacy.*

- **Anti-scientific stance.** Kinnaman notes that "millions of young Christians perceive Christianity to be in opposition to modern science" (p. 131). As "Mike" put it: "To be honest, I think that learning about science was the straw that broke the camel's back. I knew from church that I couldn't believe in both science and God, so that was it. I didn't believe in God anymore" (p. 131).

- **Intolerance.** Kinnaman points out that "one of the most pervasive perceptions among young adults [is that] the church is *exclusive.* Many in the next generation believe that Christians have an insider-outsider mentality that is always ready to bar the door to [others]. This flies in the face of [many youths'] collective values and reference points. *Tolerance* has been the cultural North Star for most of their upbringing …. And those values are more than aspirations—multiculturalism already defines the experiences and friendships of many young adults" (p. 171, emphasis in original).

- **Dogmatism.** By this term, I mean the position that certain beliefs can entertain no questions, doubts, or explorations. Dogmatism has been a problem for many thinking people for centuries, but was particularly a problem for the young adult Christians in Kinnaman's study, fully half of whom said that it was mostly or completely true of them to say that "I don't feel that I can ask my most pressing life questions in church" (p. 190).

Thus, there is certainly a vacuum in moral authority, as increasing numbers of young adults distance themselves from their churches because of the issues I have noted above. However, as it happens, the reasons that young adults increase the distance between themselves and their churches are some of the very reasons why these same adults might be attracted to Freemasonry—*if only these adults knew that these aspects of Freemasonry existed*:

- **Motivation by the positive.** Freemasonry motivates its members by holding out the hope of personal improvement, greater knowledge, and help in becoming a mature, capable human being (which is, after all, part of the symbolism inherent in the Masonic journey from Apprentice, through Fellow, to Master). There is no motivation by fear in Freemasonry proper.

- **Depth times two.** When Freemasonry functions as it ought to, Masonic symbolism is not only explained, but its application to one's life is illuminated, through the process of quality Masonic education. The Mason is also expected to know a great deal about his Craft—expectations that will only rise as Masonry resurges.

- **Pro-scientific attitude.** From the Middle Chamber lecture to our celebration of Masons' roles in founding the Royal Society in England, Freemasonry has demonstrated for centuries an affinity with the sciences.

- **Tolerance.** One of the basic tenets of our profession, as Freemasons, is "brotherly love," by which, as the Monitors teach us, "we are taught to regard the human race (or species) as one family." Masons are not to take religion, politics, race, ethnicity, national origin, social status, or other such irrelevant factors into account when it comes to selecting members or their own officers. While Freemasons in some regions are better at observing this standard than others, proper practice of this principle (rather than intolerance) is central to Freemasonry.

- **Openness.** There is little dogmatism in Freemasonry proper—because there is simply little dogma in the first place, beyond the assertion of the Fatherhood of God, the Brotherhood of Man, and the tenets of brotherly love, relief, and truth. As principles, these teachings are life-changing; however, as statements of dogma, there is simply not much here. Masonry does not permit the discussion of partisan politics or sectarian religion in its lodges. With the banishment of these topics for discussion, there simply is not much room for dogmatism to take hold. Even the rich body of Masonic symbolism is largely left to individual, non-binding interpretation.

Thus, *if Freemasons make the effort to communicate these aspects of the Fraternity to American young adults*, Masonry has the opportunity to step into the gap of moral leadership created as these adults have distances themselves from their churches.

Am I suggesting that Freemasonry become a substitute religion for these people? Nothing of the kind. Rather, I am suggesting that Freemasonry can provide a moral and intellectual framework for these people's spiritual development. In turn, this may well help these young adults either to return to their original houses of worship, to find other religious organizations that are more suited to them, or to form their own independent approaches to their personal spiritual development.

Let us say that Freemasons avail themselves of these opportunities, and that Masonry does indeed resurge—and to a strength greater than any previous peak. Just how many Masons would that be?

How Large Could Resurgent Freemasonry Become?

Let's look at the facts.

Look at Masonic membership in the United States, not in terms of absolute numbers, but in terms of the proportion of the American population who are eligible to become Freemasons in regular lodges.

At the post-World War One peak, in 1928 (just before membership figures dropped through the floor during the Great Depression; see Appendix A), the United States had a population of 120.5 million people. I liberally estimate the minimally eligible pool in any given year (males, aged 20-74) at about 32.5% of the total population,[3] which in this year

---

3   Yes, I know that there are three issues that some people will have this this method. The minimum age would have likely been 21 in 1928, and 74 would have been an old age for an EA in 1928; I am just trying to

would have been 39.2 million. This means that the 3.3 million American Masons that year comprised about **8.4%** of the minimally eligible pool of adult males.

At the post-World War Two peak, in 1954, the U.S. had a population of 163 million. The minimally eligible pool would have been 52.98 million people. This means that the 3.96 million American Masons that year comprised about **7.5%** of the minimally eligible pool of adult males.

Now, I am not remotely suggesting that we think of initiating anything like the 7.5% to 8.4% of the minimally eligible pool of adult males in the U.S. The consensus of opinion seems to be that the post-World War One membership peak was in part due to the boosterism and Babbittry of the period—to which Freemasonry's reputation as an elite fraternity of quality would be appealing—and the desire of returning troops to gain again the sense of camaraderie they had in the armed services. The consensus of opinion attributes the post-World War Two membership to much the same factors.

But we don't want men to become Freemasons for those reasons. Masonry is not one big business-networking opportunity. And although we are a fellowship, we are a fellowship with a mission to improve one's moral and spiritual character.

---

keep the same method for all years in my statistical models, including the present, when we initiate often at 19, and many 74-year-olds are spry.

Much more importantly, in 1928 and 1954, I am including the entire American male population even though, in reality, Black men would have been excluded from most (A)F&AM Grand Lodges in the U.S. Why not adjust for that? I prefer not to even appear to legitimize the blatant racism of that period in my statistical models.

So what would be reasonable here? What proportion of men are seeking moral and spiritual improvement, even enlightenment?

The social science data on the proportion of such people in the population is rather skimpy. We are left to our own devices to make an estimate here.

Let's say **5%**. One in twenty of all the men in the minimally eligible pool. It's just a feeling, but it feels all right to me (the ultimate in subjective criteria, I know). This is a lot less than either the 8.4% of the pool that we had at the post-World War One peak, or the 7.5% of the pool that we had at the post-World War Two peak.

As this book goes to press in mid-August 2017, the U.S. Census Bureau estimates the American population to number 328.3 million (see the population clock at www.census.gov). This suggests a minimally eligible pool of about 106.7 million men. Five percent of this number would be **5.3 million Masons** — almost five times the number of Masons that we actually had at year-end 2016, according to the Masonic Service Association of North America (n.d. [ca. 2017]); as of that time, there were 1.1 million American Masons, comprising about 1.06% of the eligible pool (see Appendix A).

How can this possibly be? Five percent is so much smaller a proportion of the pool than what we had after either of the two World Wars! The answer to that is very simple. At the risk of mentioning the obvious, the United States is a much, much larger country than it was back then.

We will go into the answers to that question in Chapter 6. Right now, what needs to be clear is the following:

- Freemasonry could be far stronger in its membership number than it is today, due to the size of the American population.

- This greater number of Freemasons in the U.S. can be attained without sacrificing quality. (In fact, it can best be obtained by *increasing* the quality of our Petitioners.) We can attain this strength—a strength much *greater* than we had in the membership peaks after the two World Wars—while initiating a much *lower* proportion of the adult male population.

Could We Really Do This?

5.3 million American Masons. Five times the number of Masons we have today. Could we really do this?

Of course we could. We have done it before.

Consider the revival of the Craft in the U.S. after the anti-Masonic period of American history. The growth of the Fraternity during that period was truly astonishing. The case of Masonry in New York State—the location of the Morgan incident itself—is particularly instructive in this regard.

The reader may recall that, in 1826, the former Mason-turned-anti-Mason William Morgan disappeared, an event that many supposed was the result of Masonic skullduggery. Following this, the United States entered an extended period now known as the Anti-Masonic Era. Lodges were sacked by mobs, and multitudes of Masons abandoned the Fraternity. The first time that a "third party" had any real influence in American politics was when the Anti-Masonic Party was formed in 1828; it lasted until 1836, and the Anti-Masonic Era as a whole lasted until 1840, causing depredations to American Freemasonry. As the historian Jasper Ridley has described it, "in New York state there were 480 lodges and 20,000 members in 1825, the year before Morgan disappeared; by 1835 there were only 75 lodges with 3,000 active members" (Ridley, 1999/2001, p. 186)—a reduction in membership of 85% in ten years.

But it is the recovery from the Anti-Masonic Era that most invites our attention here. Masonry began to recover in 1840. By 1856, the Grand Lodge of New York had 19,316 members (a *543% increase* in the 21 years since 1835); by 1863, two years into the American Civil War, New York had 33,320 Masons (Singer & Lang, 1981, p. 263)—an increase of over 72% in barely seven years.

Over the next decade, New York Freemasonry exploded. Membership in 1873 was 79,349 (Singer & Lang, 1981, p. 263)—an increase of 138% in just ten years. In succeeding decades, New York Freemasonry grew much larger. For instance, in 1922—the year when Lord Carnarvon and Howard Carter discovered King Tut's tomb—there were 286,594 Freemasons in New York (Grand Secretary's report within *Annual Reports*, May 2016, p. 8).

Yes, in the late 19th and early 20th centuries, this growth rate took 59 years to accomplish. However, we could accomplish this growth (or more) much more quickly in the 21st century. The facts of our circumstances in the early 21st century bear me out.

Consider the means of mass communication available during the period 1863 to 1922. For most of this period, the print newspaper or magazine was the cutting edge of mass communication technology. Radio only became available to the American masses near the end of this period, with the founding of the Radio Corporation of America (RCA) in 1919, the year after the end of the First World War. Motion pictures were certainly popular during the last 19 years of this period—every one of these films being silent, of course, and in black-and-white.

Now consider where we are today. Obviously, we have television (including Public Access Television, a resource of which few if any Grand Lodges or Particular Lodges avail themselves). But most especially, we have the Internet, where, in 2016: you can post online videos that you have shot on your smartphone; you can have a YouTube or Vimeo online video channel all your own; you can have a regular podcast—an Internet 'radio' show, if you will; you can publicize all such productions effectively by Facebook and Twitter. Basically, anyone—a Grand Lodge, a Particular Lodge, even just an individual Mason—can reach an audience of one million people in 2016 with substantially less effort than it took to reach one thousand people in 1922.

Yes, it takes some technical expertise. (Go get a moderately nerdy member of DeMolay, the Rainbow, or Triangle on board, and you're set.) Yes, it takes a little savvy about publicity. But in a world where people obtain millions of views on YouTube for videos of themselves playing video games, or cavorting with puppies and kittens, it just cannot be that hard to attract a sizeable audience of people interested in spiritual growth, moral development, and intellectual stimulation.[4]

---

[4] Case in point: as of June 2016, the online video channel with the most subscribers on YouTube is owned by a 26-year-old who posts jokey,

The bottom line: What the technologically primitive New York Freemasons of the mid-19th to early 20th centuries took nearly 60 years to accomplish—an eightfold-and-more increase in membership—we technologically enriched American Masons of the 21st century should be able to accomplish in much less time. It really is just that simple. It is not financially costly, either.

It now becomes a matter of will and effort. How much of that can we muster, on behalf of our Fraternity?

---

largely vulgar videos of himself playing video games. Over the course of six years, his videos have amassed over 12 billion—that's 12 billion with a *b*—views; he has 44 million subscribers on YouTube, and, for what it's worth, grosses about $12 million annually from advertising and sponsorship deals (Grossman, 2016b, pp. 54, 56). Surely some well-executed video channels by the inheritors of the Western Mystery Tradition could at least *approach* something like that kind of a following!

4

Our Obligation to
Make Masonry Resurge

Unless American Masons make a serious course correction, Free and Accepted Masons in the United States will become virtually extinct within the lifetimes of the men we are now initiating. (See Chapter 6, "American Freemasonry Today," for details.)

Some brethren have responded to this idea with the notion that there would be no problem for them if Freemasons became much smaller in number, or even became extinct. Some said that the essence of Freemasonry itself—that is, the quest for light—would always endure, in some expression. Some echoed a sentiment that I have long heard expressed, that there are already too many men initiated into Masonry, without the ideals of the Craft ever really penetrating into their hearts, so losing those brethren would be no real loss to the Fraternity—hence, we need not focus on increasing the number of initiations.

I beg to differ with these perspectives. My position is that **Freemasons in our era have *a moral obligation* to build Freemasonry by initiating more strong candidates than we ever have over the last half-century.** Building Freemasonry in this way is not just "a good thing": it is a matter of responsibility and duty.

To establish this point, let me ask this seemingly simple question:

What is Freemasonry *for*?

In large part, Freemasonry is about personal transformation. The scope of that task is nothing to be underestimated. But is that it? Or is there something even beyond that, as the purpose of Freemasonry?

Ponder that question for a moment. We'll be returning to it. But first we need to consider what Freemasonry teaches—that is, its principle tenets.

The Tenets of Freemasonry

Every Freemason hears at his initiation as an Entered Apprentice that the "principal tenets of our profession" are "those truly commendable virtues, Brotherly Love, Relief, and Truth."

But what, really, is a "tenet"?

Webster's Third New International Dictionary tells us that the principal meaning of "tenet" is "a principle, dogma, belief, or doctrine generally held to be true; [especially] one held in common by members of an organization, group, movement, or profession."

Implicit in this idea is that the organization wishes to see its tenets *spread*, and be observed widely. Professional organizations want to see their tenets observed by all such professionals. (So it is that the American Psychological Association wants all psychological scientists to follow certain ethical guidelines in conducting experiments, or carrying on the practice of psychotherapy.) Religious organizations wish to see the world adopt their beliefs—even if those beliefs involve toleration for others' beliefs. Political organizations want their political principles to be implemented throughout society.

So, what are we really saying when we say that that our tenets as Freemasons are "brotherly love, relief, and truth"?

We are implying that *everyone* should show brotherly love, render relief, act in truthfulness, and seek truth.

Think about it. If we continue to let Freemasonry shrink, let alone die out, in my opinion, we are failing in our obligation to uphold these tenets, for a very simple reason: without the Fraternity there to promulgate the tenets, these values become that much weaker in society. In essence, we would be consenting to the weakening of these values in our world. So, if we wish to *follow* these tenets, we must build up the Fraternity that *holds* these tenets dear.

Look at it this way. The tenets of our profession are not just for the personal benefits of Masons. From the beginning of at least the Grand Lodge era of Freemasonry, Freemasons have demonstrated publicly that they understood the wisdom of rolling out brotherly love, relief, and a concern with truth to society at large.

Brotherly Love

What is Brotherly Love? It goes far beyond having good fellowship in one's Lodge. As the Monitors put it, "By the exercise of Brotherly Love, we are taught to regard the human race (or species) as one family." Much of this is expressed in private, but there have been some spectacular examples known to the public as well. Masons looking out for each other across the lines of battle have long been the stuff of shining moments in Masonic history, including during the American War Between the States (Halleran, 2010). But the Masonic tenet of brotherly love, and the ethic of meeting on the level, go beyond expressions from one individual to another.

Think of the framers of the Declaration of Independence and the Constitution of the United States, two documents drenched in Masonic ideals. As the framers of the Declaration of Independence put it, among the truths that they held to be self-evident, the first was that "all Men are created equal." The Constitution forbids the United States to grant titles of nobility, and forbids officers or agents of the federal government from accepting titles of nobility from foreign governments or their leaders (Article I, Section 9, final paragraph). In the era when the Constitution was written, this was a huge issue: the existence of a titled aristocracy divided European societies into Nobility versus Commoners—something that the framers of the Constitution were determined not to perpetuate in their new country. This is a good example of Masonic ideals affecting an entire society. But we can go farther.

Think of U.S. President Harry S. Truman, then Past Grand Master of Masons in Missouri, ending racial segregation in the Armed Forces through Executive Order 9981 in 1948. Yes, Truman was acting in his official capacity as the President, not as a Freemason. But surely his judgment in this matter was informed by his Masonry. Truman's action wound up having a great impact on American society, and was a great step towards the ideal of an integrated society.

Would we not want future leaders in this country to be informed by *their* Masonry? That would be difficult, if Freemasonry were to be nearly extinct. And if we let Freemasons disappear from American society, are we not actually failing in our obligation to follow the tenet of Brotherly Love?

Relief

As the Monitors teach us, "to relieve the distressed is a duty incumbent on all men." I am thinking of many examples of quiet but vital charity rendered by the lodges I have attended over the years. But expressions of the Masonic tenet of Relief can be found on a much larger scale, as well. In England, I am thinking of 18th century expressions like the founding of the Royal Masonic School for Girls and the Royal Masonic School for Boys; I am also thinking of 21st century expressions, like the pledge by London Freemasons from Metropolitan Grand Lodge to donate US$2.8 million for an air ambulance (Hodapp, 2016; "London Freemasons," 2015). In the United States, of course, the charity that funds the Shriners Hospitals is legendary. It is often forgotten that New York Masons founded in 1809 one of the first free, nonsectarian elementary schools in New York City (Singer & Lang, 1981, Chapter 13). Over the course of a decade, this school turned out to be an important step in establishing what is today the nation's largest public school system.

But there are also times when Masons have structured relief on a societal scale. The entire New Deal of U.S. President Franklin D. Roosevelt—well-known as a Mason—is arguably an extension of the Masonic tenet of Relief to a national scale. Of course, here too, FDR was acting in his official capacity as the President, not as a Freemason. But here again, FDR's judgment was doubtless informed by his Freemasonry.

Here, too, I must ask, would we not want the actions of future leaders in this country—and throughout the world!—to be informed by their Masonic values? And if we let Freemasons shrink within or even disappear from American society, are we not actually failing in our obligation to extend Relief?

Truth—Part 1: Truthfulness and Integrity

The Monitors teach us that "to be good and true is the first lesson we are taught in Masonry…. sincerity and plain dealing distinguish us." In a 21st century world where corruption is a byword on every continent, where political and business corruption has ruined the economies and politics of nations, the Masonic ideal of truth is as timely as the headlines on today's breaking news reports.

I have seen that ideal show up in many private arrangements between Masons: deals sealed with a handshake and honored without paper; disputes settled without lawsuits. It is a beautiful thing to see.

But here, too, Masons have been prominent in advancing the cause of truthfulness and integrity in society. I do not think it is a coincidence that U.S. Presidents Teddy Roosevelt and Franklin Delano Roosevelt—each a Freemason—took major steps to decrease corruption, in both the American political process and in American businesses. Here again: men acting in their elected capacities, but informed by their Masonic ideals, helped change American society for the better.

Would we *not* want more and more of this—especially given how badly this is needed, throughout the United States?

And if we let Freemasons disappear from American society, are we not actually failing in our obligation to follow and further Truthfulness?

Truth—Part 2: The Pursuit of Knowledge

But there is another way altogether in which Truth and Freemasonry have a special relationship. And here, too, Masons acting in their private and public capacities, but informed by Masonic ideals, have changed societies—and, in the course of doing that, changed the course of human history.

For centuries, Masonry has emphasized mathematics and science as a way to investigate and understand reality. The first important public document of the Grand Lodge era of Freemasonry, James Anderson's (1723/1734) *The Constitutions of the Free-Masons*, goes on for dozens of pages regarding how stonemasons from ancient times up to Anderson's era, through the use of geometry, erected the most important buildings of the ages. My point is that Anderson's document reflects the high esteem in which Freemasonry has held mathematics and geometry from the very beginning of the three centuries that we have had Grand Lodge Freemasonry.

These lessons have been passed on to Masonic initiates for centuries. Apparently, these lessons have made a difference.

The oldest existing "learned society," the Royal Society in England (founded 1660), was largely created by men who were made Freemasons in the century before the founding of the premier Grand Lodge in London—men such as Robert Moray and Christopher Wren; other Masons, including Elias Ashmole and Jean Desaguliers, were early members of the Royal Society (Bauer, 2007; Lomas, 2003).

The Royal Society was a mainstay of observational and experimental science at a crucial juncture in human history (Jacob, 2010). In our day, it funds about 600 research fellowships at any one time, and gives numerous awards to fund yet more scientific research. Beyond that, it has served as a model for learned societies all around the world (including the American Psychological Association, of which I have the honor of having been elected a Fellow myself).

In a very real sense, the Royal Society served as midwife to the birth of modern science. Here again, we see a number of Freemasons, acting in their private capacities but clearly informed by thoroughly Masonic values, doing something that has changed the course, not just of one society, but of all human civilization, for the better.

Don't we want more of this? Don't we *need* more of this? And if we let Freemasons disappear from American society, are we not actually failing in our obligation to pursue truth and knowledge?

Conclusion: What Freemasonry Is For

I've mentioned the names of some great Masons above. Seeing how they lived out their Masonic ideals leads me to a conclusion:

> **Freemasonry is *not* just about making a good man better.** It's *not* just about improving a man's life, not even just about making him a better husband, father, worker, friend, or member of his community. Yes, it is about all those things— but it is more.

Freemasonry is also about improving society. It is about improving human civilization.

And we can only do that with more, and better, Freemasons.

Freemasons have done great things in the past by following the principle tenets of their profession, by extending brotherly love, an ethic of relief, a commitment to truthfulness, and a passion for the discovery of truth, not only to other individuals, but to entire societies.

The world in general, and American society in particular, is in desperate need of a greater implementation of these tenets. In the past, Freemasons have changed the world by applying these tenets on a grand scale. That's not going to happen much more, though, if Masons become an endangered species or go extinct.

Freemasonry is worth preserving—and extending.

What we need is not fewer Masons, but more Masons who will let the values of Freemasonry soak into their souls. How do we accomplish that? That is what Part Three of this book is all about. But first, we must have a clear sense of what our current situation actually is, both in American society at large, and in American Freemasonry. These issues are the focus of Part Two of this book, which follows this chapter.

PART TWO

THE PRESENT SITUATION

5

American Society Today

There is no question that American and other Western societies could benefit from a good, strong dose of Masonic philosophy and ethics. For example, in the United States, we see today an erosion of support for the Constitution's expressly stated separation of church and state—all in direct contrast to the Masonic principles of religious toleration and neutrality.

There is a powerful and growing movement in some American states for the teaching of religious doctrines instead of scientific findings in public schools. Powerful political figures deny scientific findings that have important implications for the welfare of all human civilization. All of this is in direct contradiction to Masonic exhortations to study Nature—yes, as God's creation in the heavens and on the Earth—through such Liberal Arts and Sciences as Logic, Mathematics, and Astronomy, and, by implication, through other observational and experimental sciences, which are all dependent on observational data rather than religious or political doctrine. The Middle Chamber lecture, in all its details, is a powerful statement of both educational and political philosophy.

The very nature of our political discourse has become as distant from Masonic standards of civil, reasoned discussion as it has ever been, in the history of the American nation. Here again, powerful political figures have descended to gutter-level vulgarity in public; they sanction and even encourage personal violence by their followers against those who oppose them. And, here again, all of this violates Masonic principles of reasoned, civil discourse and mutual respect, even between those of diametrically opposed political views. What the Monitors teach us is a guide for leadership in general: "Make others to know always that a gentleman stands before them."

But it is not just in American society that one sees departures from Masonic civilizing principles. Europe as well has seen the reemergence of political parties that encourage xenophobia and violence. And in Western Europe, one notes the demise, almost what seems to be the signs of the approaching death, of traditional religious belief among the general population (see Berger et al., 2008). For example, in a 1999-2000 study of adults in Western Europe, it was found that less than half the population in France, Germany, Spain, Portugal, Denmark, and Sweden believed in a life after death; in Great Britain, France, Germany, and Sweden, about 30%-40% or more of the population held no belief in God, and were effectively atheists (Davie, 2002, pp. 6-7). This is in direct contradiction to the underlying dynamics of Anglophone Freemasonry, where reason is united with a faith in a Supreme Being.

And the trend in the United States is coming to resemble that of Western Europe. In a sample of American adults in 2014, 22% stated that they did not believe in God; this proportion rose to 30% among those adults under the age of 30 years old (Twenge et al., 2016, pp. 5, 7).

It is clear, then, that the Western world as a whole, and America in particular, need Masonic philosophy more than at any time since the ratification of the American Constitution over two centuries ago. Indeed, at least one Masonic author has taken the position that "Masonry is going to be the barrier that blocks the secularization of the world," and that "Masonry is going to be the vehicle to bring people back to God" (Livingstone, 2015).

But is Freemasonry up to the task of renewing our society? Let us briefly review the current situation in American Freemasonry.

6

American Freemasonry Today

Here is some unhappy news from the membership figures reported by the Masonic Service Association of North America ([MSANA], n.d. [ca. 2017]; see Appendix A):

- U.S. Masonic membership at year-end 2016 was the lowest it has ever been since MSANA started keeping figures in 1924. (See Figure 6-1.)

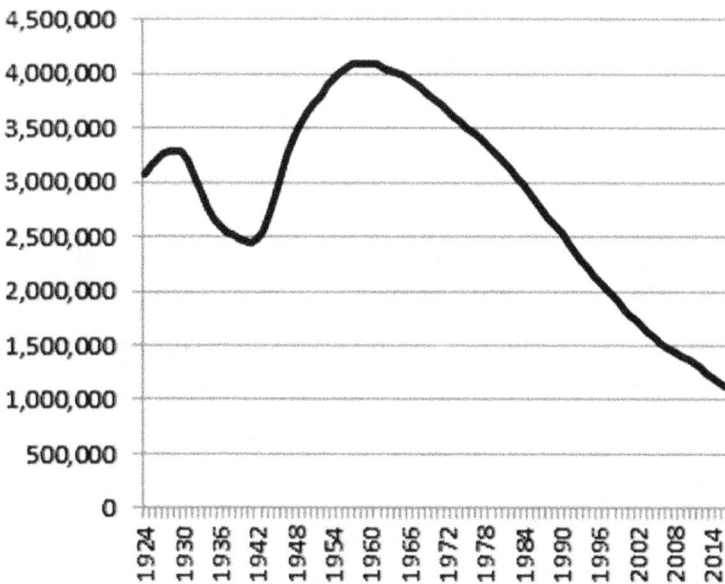

Fig. 6-1. U.S. Masonic membership, 1924-2016.

- During the 15-year period, 2002-2016, the U.S. lost 35% of its Masonic membership. (See Figure 6-2.)

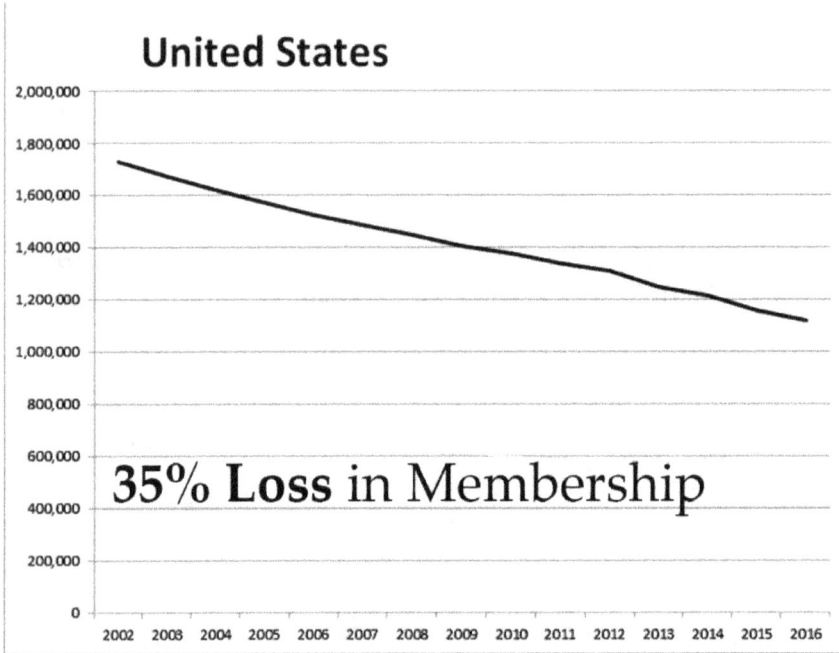

United States

35% **Loss** in Membership

Fig. 6-2. U.S. Masonic Membership, 2002-2016.

- The same trend in membership seen in the U.S. as a whole was also seen during 2002-2016 in the six largest U.S. Grand Lodges: California (Fig. 6-3), Illinois (Fig. 6-4), Indiana (Fig. 6-5), Ohio (Fig. 6-6), Pennsylvania (Fig. 6-7), and Texas (Fig. 6-8). For the record, the same holds true for the two Grand Lodges where I hold Masonic membership, Florida (Fig. 6-9) and New York (Fig. 6-10), as well as in neighboring New Jersey (Fig. 6-11).

GL California

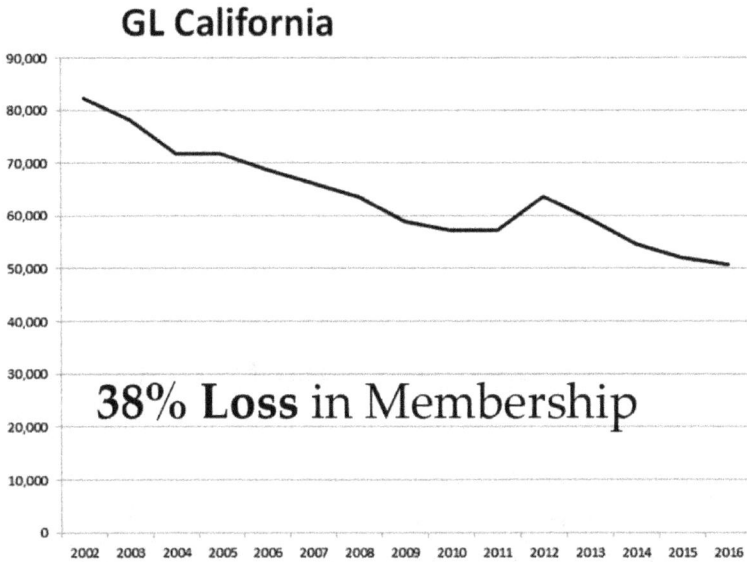

38% Loss in Membership

Fig. 6-3. GLCA Masonic Membership, 2002-2016.

GL Illinois

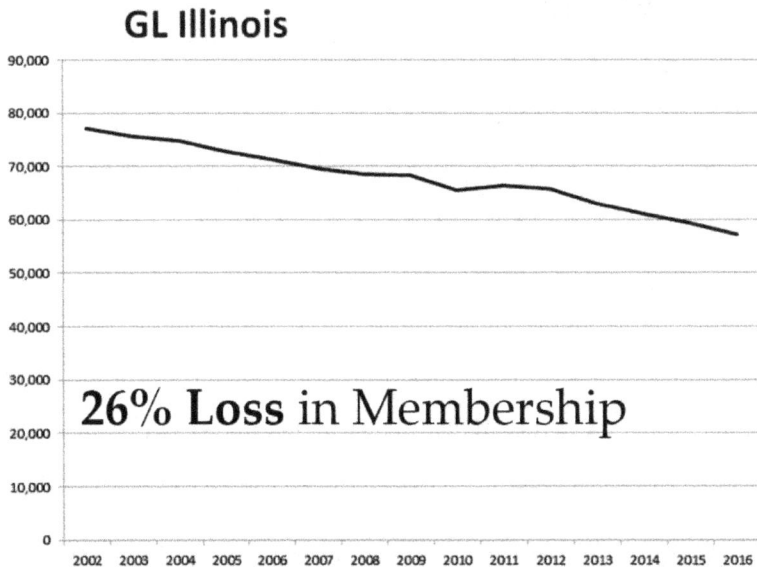

26% Loss in Membership

Fig. 6-4. GLIL Masonic Membership, 2002-2016.

GL Indiana

34% Loss in Membership

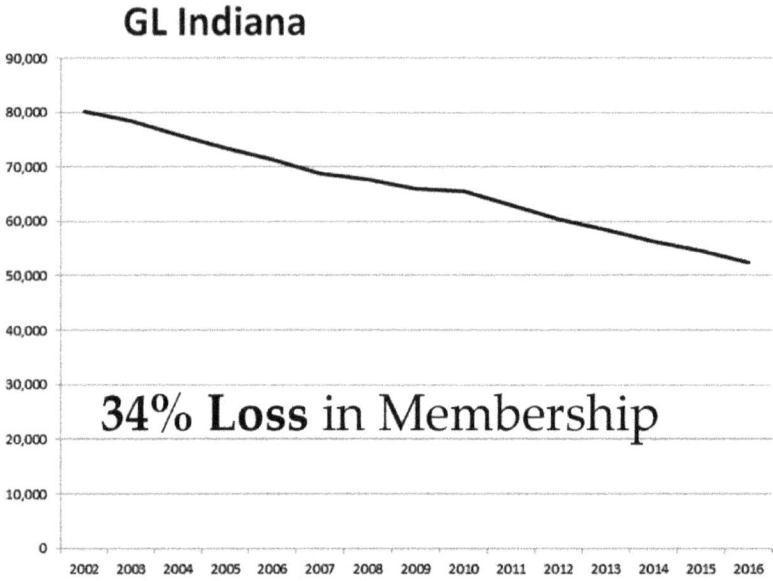

Fig. 6-5. GLIN Masonic Membership, 2002-2016.

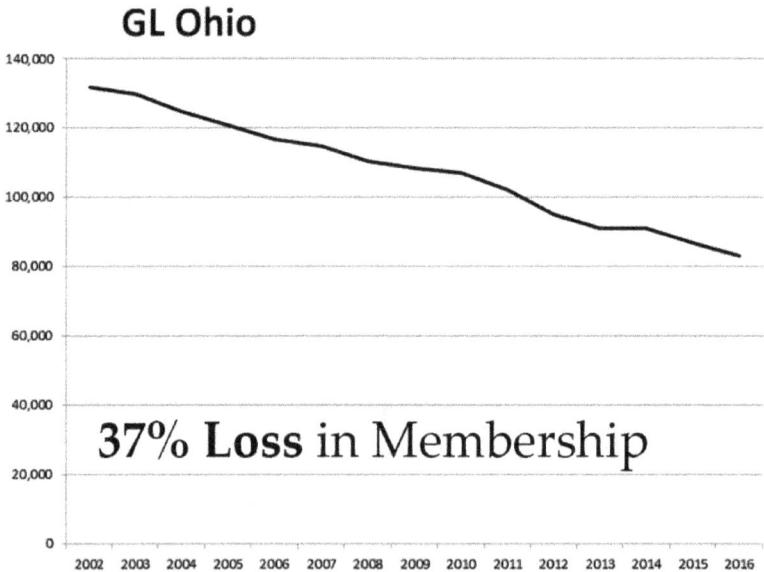

GL Ohio

37% Loss in Membership

Fig. 6-6. GLOH Masonic Membership, 2002-2016.

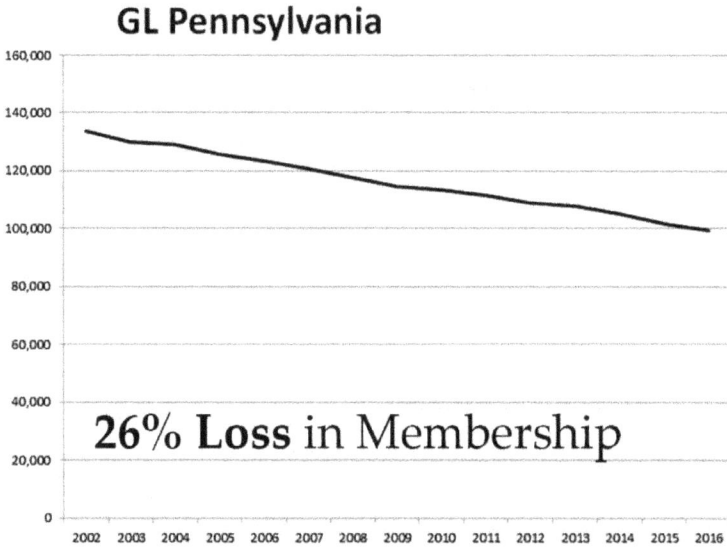

Fig. 6-7. GLPA Masonic Membership, 2002-2016.

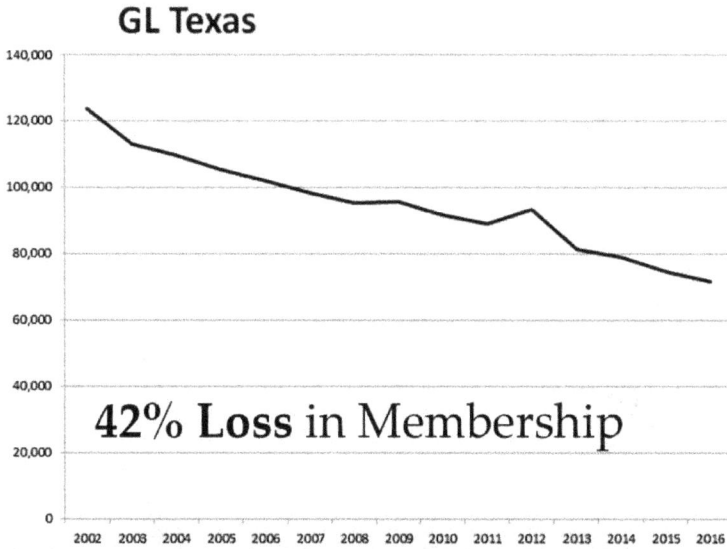

Fig. 6-8. GLTX Masonic Membership, 2002-2016.

GL Florida

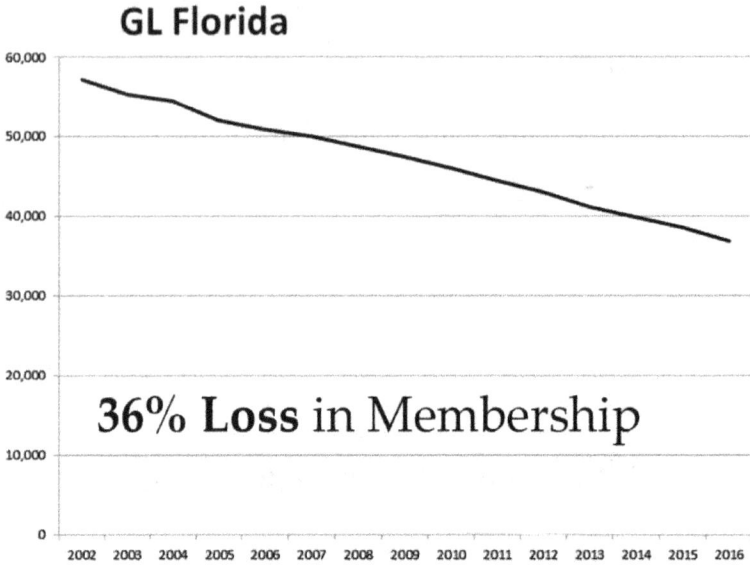

36% **Loss** in Membership

Fig. 6-9. GLFL Masonic Membership, 2002-2016.

GL New York

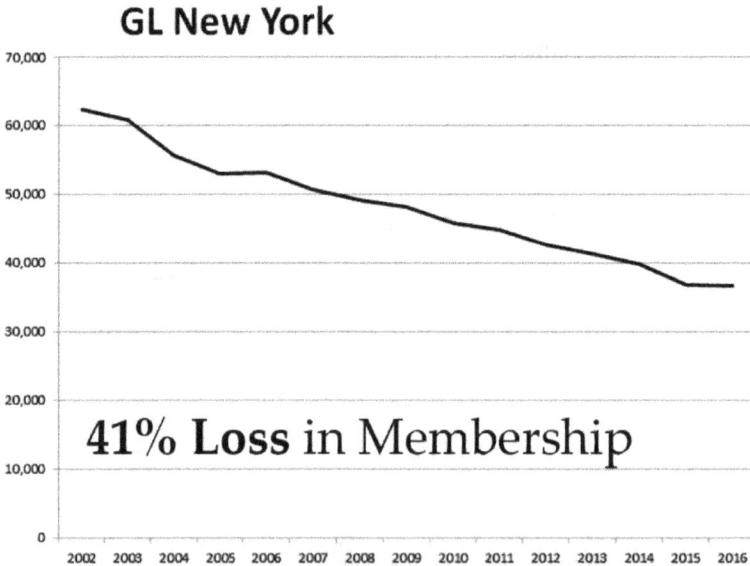

41% **Loss** in Membership

Fig. 6-10. GLNY Masonic Membership, 2002-2016.

GL New Jersey

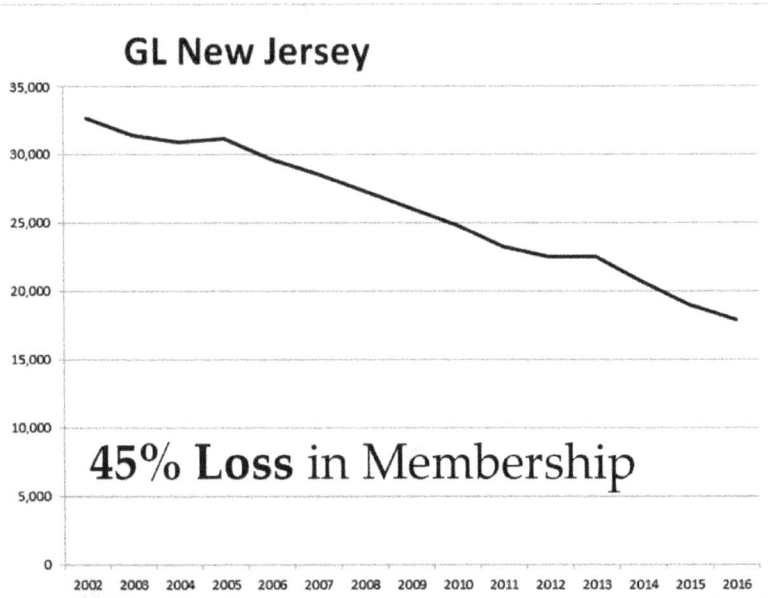

45% **Loss** in Membership

Fig. 6-11. GLNJ Masonic Membership, 2002-2016.

Where Is This All Going?

An American male born on January 1, 1997 or earlier would be eligible to petition for the degrees of Freemasonry throughout the U.S. in 2018. What will Freemasonry look like in 2060, when these brethren are in their early sixties and beyond?

If current trends continue, Masons will have slipped in nationwide membership from 1,117,781 members in 2016 to 313,744 in 2060—a drop in membership of about 72% from what we have today (Figure 6-12).[5] As far as I'm concerned, a

---

5   I simply applied a net membership decline rate of 2.8% to the period 2017 through 2060. This membership decline rate has been remarkably

drop in membership of 72% will mean that Freemasonry as we know it will have ceased to exist. In other words, if these trends continue, U.S. Freemasonry will have become virtually extinct during the lifetimes of men we are now initiating.

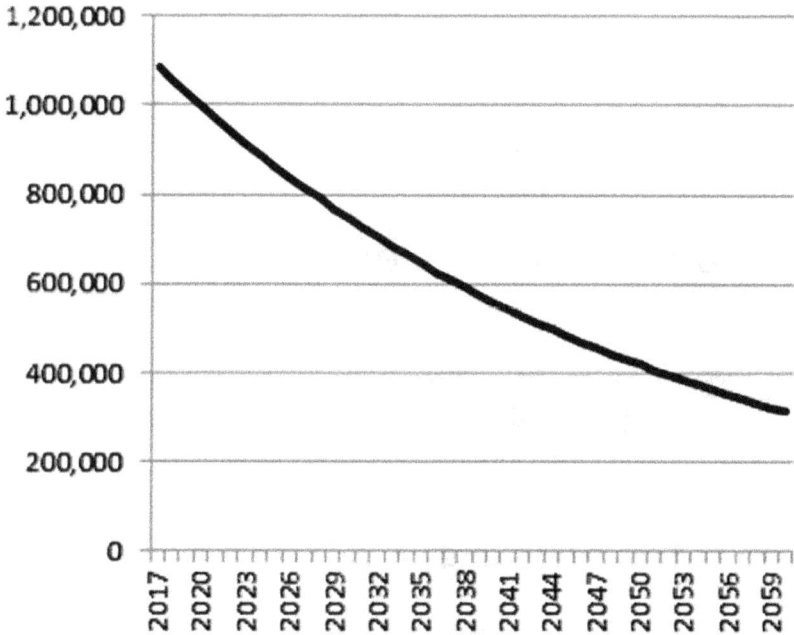

Fig. 6-12. Projected U.S. Masonic Membership, 2017-2060.

As the R∴W∴ Phillip A. Hudson stated at the 2007 Grand Communication in Florida: **"We are one generation away from extinction"** (Hudson, 2007).

---

stable: it was the median amount of membership decline seen through 2016 whether we start back 10 years, 20 years, or even 40 years.

Think what extinction would mean. We would no longer be providing initiatic experiences for men, nor the personal growth that those experiences can nurture. We would no longer exert a living, civilizing influence in society at large. Our vaunted charities might continue if they have sufficiently large endowments, but otherwise they'll be gone too. The many quiet acts of local relief and charity that our lodges do? Without lodges to do them, these acts will not occur.

But this projection is like Charles Dickens' Ghost of Christmas-Yet-to-Come: it is a future that will be, only if we continue on the path we are on.

There Are Five Major Reasons for the Masonic Membership Decline

There are many mysteries within Masonry, but the reasons for its decline in membership are not among them. I identify five major reasons for the Masonic decline that we have seen over the last six decades and more.

1. In Many Lodges, Masonry is Not Delivering What It Promises—And So Men Leave.

At present, the most important reason for membership loss is *voluntary* attrition: that is, voluntary demits, and dismissals from the Fraternity because of non-payment of dues (NPDs), typically before a man's seventh year in Freemasonry (Belton, 2001).

But why? Why do demits and NPDs actually exceed the number of initiations in many jurisdictions? My straightforward explanation: *In many lodges, Freemasonry just does not deliver what it promises.*

Why do men come to Freemasonry? Not for the sake of donating to charity or even to give service. There are many opportunities for these, and for fellowship, aside from Freemasonry.

At this point in the 21ˢᵗ century, men come to Freemasonry primarily for the sake of their own self-culture and education. **Men come to Freemasonry in order to learn about the Mystery of the universe, and to improve themselves so as to better learn that Mystery, in the company of other like-minded men.**

This is what men come to Masonry to find: a way to understand the Big Questions, a way to improve themselves so that they'll be better able to handle the Big Answers, and a social context in which they can do that with like-minded brothers. This is what Masonry, with its centuries-long reputation and its impressive initiatory ceremonies, promises them.

And then so many lodges deliver business meetings, with all the spiritual content of a phone bill. This is not the kind of experience that will bring men back to lodge month after month, year after year.

The result is that, as the MBAs among us might put it, in many lodges, Freemasonry fails to deliver on its value proposition. And so people demit, or just stop paying their dues.

2. Many Lodges Fail to Deliver Quality Masonic Education

The value of Masonic education is all too often honored in word without actually delivering it. When it is delivered in a lodge room, quite often it has been given too little preparation time in advance; in the meeting quite often it is given too little time to really have an impact, or it focuses on things that do not really change lives, like "famous Masons."

Perhaps worse, it seems that few lodges have an overall approach or framework for delivering Masonic education. The brothers hear a hodgepodge of different types of topics with no overarching order or structure to them.

In 2014, I conducted an online survey of Freemasons. Hundreds responded, mostly from the United States, and by far the single change that they most wanted to see happen in the Fraternity was the widespread implementation of quality Masonic education.

When we deliver poor Masonic education—or when we do not deliver it at all—we undercut much of the reason that men became Masons in the first place. A lack of quality Masonic education in many lodges is killing Freemasonry, one NPD at a time.

3. Very Few People Have an Accurate Idea About Freemasonry—Or Even Know That It Still Exists

Within living memory, pretty much every adult in America knew that the Freemasons existed. In 1954, Freemasons comprised about 7.8% of the adult American male population; there was 1 Mason for every 13 or 14 adult males in the U.S.

That whole picture has changed today, of course. In 2016, Masons comprised barely over 1% of adult American males;

there is only 1 Mason for about every 100 or so adult males in the U.S. Hardly anyone knows that Masonry still exists.[6]

The net result is that Masons have become close to invisible in society. One group of Masons in the American heartland, the Knights of the North, described "the loss of ... knowledge of the Craft in the public consciousness" in our day:

> In less than one hundred years after the birth of the first Grand Lodge [in 1717], virtually every man, woman and child in the Western world knew who Freemasons were and what the Order stood for....
>
> Yet, sixty years after [World War II], fewer and fewer people in society knew what a Freemason was, or that the fraternity still existed. (Knights of the North, 2006, pp. 8, 10)

No wonder, then, that the R∴W∴ Phillip A. Hudson (2007, p. 273) stated this during his Grand Oration in Florida:

> The average person does not have a true concept of who we are or what we stand for.... In today's time, would any worthy man want to become a member of a Fraternity he knows nothing about?

---

6   "But what about Dan Brown and *National Treasure*?" As I write these words, that media hoopla ended over a dozen years ago. For a more extended consideration of this issue, see Koltko-Rivera (2018, Aug. 7; begin at about the 7:14 mark).

4. We May Be Bringing In Some Inappropriate Candidates

Of those gentlemen whom we do initiate, we may be bringing in gentlemen who are not, in fact, interested in what Freemasonry is really about, which certainly includes intensive self-discovery and self-improvement. Indeed, we may be bringing in "gentlemen" who are not actual gentlemen at all.

The Most Worshipful Grand Master of Masons in New York, Jeffrey M. Williamson (now P∴G∴M∴), had this to say in his first St. John's Day address, as reported in *The Empire State Mason Magazine*:

> In recent times, a petition for membership was eagerly and hastily presented to any man who showed even the slightest interest in our fraternity. Prior to his acceptance, the prospect had little or no education as to what our expectations might be for him on his journey through Freemasonry, or what his expectations might be for us. (Williamson, 2016, p. 5)

This is not a system calculated to bring in only the best. The results are almost predictable. Some men who become Masons become easily bored even at the most dynamic lodges, simply because they are not that interested in personal growth in the first place. Even worse, this process can even bring charlatans and criminals into the lodge, weakening the entire Craft; as then-Grand Master Williamson stated:

> [Unworthy] men now disguised as Master Masons have slowly infiltrated into our beloved Institution. They have inflicted their reprehensible and law-breaking misconduct on innocent and

trusting Brothers and their families. The Proctor's Docket is full of troublemakers, mischief-makers, and criminals. (Williamson, 2016, p. 6)

I have observed the same phenomenon in other Grand Lodges as well. Anecdotal evidence suggests that the problem is widespread throughout the American Craft.

5. Anti-Masonic Propaganda Discourages the Honest in Heart from Investigating Freemasonry

The Masonic Service Association of North America (2016a) has stated the following:

> We believe that the public's perception and opinion of Freemasonry can be summarized briefly in the following ways:
>
> 1. *Confused.* Are the Masons a fraternity, a religious organization, or an alternative religion?
>
> 2. *Mistaken.* Only grandfathers could be in such an old-fashioned association as Freemasonry.
>
> 3. *Oblivious.* People are not even aware Masonry still exists.

As damaging as each of these public perceptions are to the survival of the Fraternity, there is a fourth perception, shared by a sizable minority of the public, that presents its own special challenges. I describe it this way:

> **4.** *Delusional.* Some people believe that Masonry is a Satanic, devil-worshipping conspiracy bent on enslaving humanity.

On April 25, 2016, I conducted a review of: (1) the first 100 Web pages found in an online (Google) search of the term "Freemasonry," and (2) the first 100 videos found by searching the same term on YouTube. The results were quite troubling:

- One-fifth (20%) of the top-ranked web page results were clearly anti-Masonic in nature.

- Fully half (51%) of the top-ranked YouTube video results were clearly anti-Masonic in nature.

Here are the titles of some representative examples of the anti-Masonic web pages:

- "The Aim of Freemasonry is the Triumph of Communism."

- "Freemasons – The silent destroyers. Deist religious cult."

- "Freemasons Exposed!" (Description: "The gods of the Freemasonry lodge [*sic*] are Egyptian gods.")

- "Freemasonry: Midwife to an Occult Empire." (Description: "Evidence that the higher Masonic degrees conceal the true nature of Freemasonry as a Satanic religion.")

So there you have it. Freemasonry is supposedly a Satanic conspiracy, bent on totalitarian rule. If anything, these themes are picked up even more sharply in the anti-Masonic YouTube videos, of which these titles are representative:

- "Join freemasonry [*sic*] & lose your soul (proof)."

- "Secrets of Freemasonry found in masonic books." (Description: "Lucifer is the god of Freemasonry and other facts written by high ranking masons in their own books that are found in libraries ....")

- "The Secret Agenda of High Level Freemasonry."

- "Illuminati The Freemasonry [*sic*] and Zionism – The Master Plan to Rule the World."

- "Why Won't Celebrities Tell Their Illuminati Freemasonry Secrets?"

- "Freemasonry: A Jewish Luciferian Cult (a rare daring investigation)."

- "Baphomet is the 'God' of Freemasonry."

- "Freemasonry, Masonic Lodge and the Shriners Are Not Compatible with Biblical Christianity."

- "Lucifer Worshippers Exposed!!! Plotting SOON World takeover!!! Illuminati – Jesuits – Freemasonry."

The nine videos above had a combined total of 804,296 views on the date of my review. (Individual videos ranged from 5,508 to 191,882 views.)

But the videos above are low-performing pikers in comparison to the most-popular such videos. Some anti-Masonic videos in the YouTube top-ranked 100 have had *over one million views—apiece.* (The #1-ranked video on "Freemasonry" contended that the Fraternity is an ongoing indoctrination into Satanism. This video alone had *over two million views* at the time of my survey. Its title: "Watch THIS Before Joining Freemasonry!")

The upshot of all this is that when a potential candidate goes online to find out information about the Fraternity, a substantial proportion of what he encounters will be, not just misinformed inaccuracies, but melodramatic delusions of the most lurid sort. Should he look for online *videos* on the topic—the preferred method of the Millennial generation and Generation Z, it seems—then the search for truth may be aborted at the very beginning, because of the flood of highly developed but delusional, bizarre falsehoods about Freemasonry that are easily available on the Internet.

We must not tolerate this any longer. We must directly counter the grotesque and often sickening lies told about Freemasonry—lies that I believe keep many good men from the Fraternity.

I have good reason to believe this—because *I* was one of those men who were kept from the Fraternity by anti-Masonic propaganda. My petition to a Masonic lodge was put off by perhaps as much as twenty years, as a result of reading the false accusations against Freemasonry advanced by the notorious Stephen Knight in his popular book *The Brotherhood.* Sometimes I think about what I could have accomplished as a Mason in those twenty years. We all should think about the many men who might otherwise have been truly great Masons, had they not been led astray by anti-Masonry—an anti-Masonry that we have often abstained from responding to.

To summarize: We have become numerically a much weaker Fraternity in the U.S. because—speaking of many lodges, not all—we simply became lazy; on top of that, the world changed around us, and we failed to respond:

- Many, many lodges paid less and less attention to the Masonic mission of moral and spiritual improvement, in favor of the much easier mission of providing superficial fellowship and charity. Many, many lodges let the quality of the Lodge experience, including the provision of quality Masonic education, go by the boards.

- We allowed Freemasonry to pass out of the public consciousness, and become more or less invisible.

- We grasped at anyone who showed the slightest interest in the Fraternity, rather than exercising better practices with interested parties and Petitioners.

- We ignored the tsunami of anti-Masonic information that came with the advent of the public Internet, now over a generation ago. Basically, we all but abandoned the field to the ancient enemies of Masonry: Ignorance, Prejudice, and Greed.[7]

The chapters in Part III of this book contain my Recommendations for how to address each of these issues.

---

[7] Sharp Masons will know that to which I refer here. These three qualities are abundantly available in anti-Masonry: Ignorance of what Masonry really is; Prejudice, often based on religious grounds, regarding what Masonry stands for; and Greed, as shown by the many who have sought to turn a dollar by selling salacious fictions about the Masons.

PART THREE

THE PLAN

7

Who Shall Bring About the Resurgence of Freemasonry?

I hope that you, the reader, have been inspired by the material in Part One, regarding the kind of Fraternity that we could build and help to flourish, and the Masonic civilization that then might grow in America and throughout the world. I also hope that you are encouraged by the material that I presented in Part One regarding the potential the Freemasonry in America actually has for growth.

In addition, I hope that you have been steeled for future efforts by the warnings that I have offered in Part Two. Truly may it be said that our Fraternity needs our efforts more than ever—and that the world needs Freemasonry more than ever, as well.

Now, in Part Three, we take action.

We shall accomplish the resurgence of Freemasonry, if at all, by making progress on several different fronts. I describe the efforts required in later chapters, in terms of five symbolic tasks that involve building or repairing "structures"; the remaining chapters of this book go over these tasks in detail. Within each of those chapters, I describe specific actions that can be taken by each of these four types of individuals, whom I call "The Four Men of Masonry":

1. the individual Freemason;

2. the Worshipful Master of a Particular Lodge;

3. the R∴W∴ District Deputy Grand Master; and,

4. the Most Worshipful Grand Master.

It is to these four men that I turn our attention for the remainder of this chapter. For it is not enough to specify what actions must be taken: these actions must be owned as the responsibility of specific individuals.

The First Man: The Individual Freemason

The individual Freemason—which is to say, *you*—is the man upon whom all the weight really rests for making the resurgence of Freemasonry happen. In the remaining chapters of this book, I give plenty of specific Recommendations for what an individual Mason can do, regardless of whether or not the Master of his lodge, his District Deputy Grand Master, or his Grand Master do anything along these lines *at all*.

Over half a century ago, the MWPGM Dwight Smith of Indiana wrote that one of the pitfalls of Freemasonry as we have been practicing it is centralization, an approach which he described as follows: "Pattern Freemasonry after Washington bureaucracy. Let nothing be done modestly by an individual or a Lodge; do everything on [the] state or national level the super-duper way" (D. Smith, quoted in Knights of the North, 2006, .pdf p. 6).

Although I do describe actions that a Grand Master or a DDGM can take, many of my Recommendations in the next five chapters of this book are about what an individual can do, or his lodge, to further the resurgence of Freemasonry.

Let me be clear about this. *In very large part, the resurgence of Freemasonry depends on what the individual Mason does.* It really is just that simple.

Those readers who are not the Worshipful Masters of their lodges, District Deputy Grand Masters, or Grand Lodge officers, are welcome to move on to the next five chapters at this point, where I discuss specifics of what the rank-and-file Mason can do. (On the other hand, if you think that you might someday *be* one of these officers, then I suggest that you give the rest of this chapter a careful read.)

The Second Man: The Worshipful Master

The Worshipful Master of a Particular Lodge can do a great deal to further the resurgence of Freemasonry. Well has it been said that "all Masonry is local" (Knights of the North, 2006, .pdf p. 30). Worshipful Masters can perform three types of activities to further the Masonic resurgence.

First, the Worshipful Master can inspire the members of his lodge *en masse* to engage in the work of building the Fraternity. Some might think that this might not amount to much. The reality is quite different.

As a thought experiment, let us say that, in any given lodge, the Worshipful Master's exhortations, and the various sessions of Masonic education held under his direction, cumulatively inspire *only two brothers* of the lodge to focus some significant effort on the Masonic resurgence. Given that we have roughly 9,700 lodges in the United States as of mid-2016, even if this relatively poor result for a Worshipful Master's teachings were replicated nationwide, we would have about *19,400 Masons* in the country making significant efforts to further the work! That is a huge amount of human effort.

Second, the leadership of a lodge can set policies and pro-cedures for the lodge as a whole to follow. This is important for each of the tasks I describe later to further the Masonic re-surgence. For example, it is particularly easy to see the im-portance of lodge leadership in directing the preparation of would-be Petitioners, as well as the investigation of Petition-ers.

Third, a Worshipful Master can help lead his lodge to cre-ate, organize, and hold group events (such as a lodge dinner, or a Masonic Open House). These sorts of events can have a major effect on the growth of a lodge. Let me illustrate this with a personal example.

Like many men interested in Freemasonry, my first en-counter with a lodge was at such an event: a dinner open to members of the public, held monthly at Winter Park Lodge No. 239 in Florida. I found the event to be well-prepared, with a good speaker; I found the event to be well-attended, with many brethren bringing their spouses, children, and friends. I found the lodge officers to be well-prepared to deal with someone like me, who essentially walked in off the street, full of questions.

Let's put all the preparation and so forth to the side, and consider hard results. Was this event actually a *success*, in terms of furthering the Masonic resurgence?

Well—I'm a Mason today, am I not?

I assure you, if that first encounter with a lodge had *not* gone well, then I probably would *not* be a Freemason today. That is just the blunt truth of the matter.

All these types of efforts—inspiring lodge members, set-ting policies and procedures, and creating events—are im-portant in furthering the resurgence of Freemasonry.

The Third Man: The District Deputy Grand Master

The Masonic District—a group of Particular Lodges that are usually within a specific geographical region of the territory under the jurisdiction of the Grand Lodge—also has a role in furthering the Masonic resurgence. The District Deputy Grand Master (DDGM) can pursue three types of activities to further this resurgence.

First, the DDGM can train groups of rank-and-file Masons in how to engage in the work of building the Fraternity. In many Jurisdictions, a DDGM addresses his District's Masons in two separate annual meetings: the official visit to a Particular Lodge, and the official Meeting or Conference of all Masons within the District. These are two powerful occasions during which a DDGM can instruct Masons in how to engage one or more of the tasks involved in helping Freemasonry resurge.

Second, the DDGM can train the leadership of Particular Lodges in how to engage their lodge members in furthering the work of the Masonic resurgence. In some Grand Lodges, it is standard procedure for a DDGM to have a private discussion with a lodge's Worshipful Master, as well as a training session for the line leadership of the lodge (the Worshipful Master, Senior and Junior Wardens, and Senior and Junior Deacons), in connection with the DDGM's official visit to a lodge. In addition, it is not unusual, before the annual District Conference, for the DDGM to meet with the line leadership of all the Particular Lodges in the District. Each of these occasions is an excellent time for the DDGM to train lodge officers in how to help their lodges further the Masonic resurgence.

Third, the DDGM is in a unique position to *coordinate* the work of lodges in his District. For example, depending on the

District, it might be preferable to have all the lodges in the District to hold Masonic Open Houses on the same date; on the other hand, it might be preferable to have the lodges distribute the dates for their Open Houses throughout the year. The DDGM can coordinate all of this.

The Fourth Man: The Grand Master

The Most Worshipful Grand Master is uniquely situated to make things happen within his jurisdiction. There are five types of activities that a Grand Master can perform to further the resurgence of Freemasonry.

1. Make and announce the decision.

First, and by far the most important action of all, the Grand Master can *make and announce the decision* to make the full-scale resurgence of Freemasonry a central—perhaps *the* central—emphasis of his tenure as Grand Master.

Making a decision and announcing it will greatly increase the likelihood that this decision will be carried out. It is taking a stand. It is setting a public agenda. It is putting the Craft on notice throughout the Grand Master's jurisdiction. And, by doing these things, the Grand Master will be fulfilling one of the most important duties of a leader.

2. Obtain commitments from his likely successors.

Second, the Grand Master can not only make this commitment himself, but he can also obtain (non-binding) commitments from the rest of the elected Grand Line to do the same during *their* respective tenures as Grand Master. **Such a**

Grand Lodge will make *major* progress towards the resurgence of Freemasonry within its Jurisdiction.

The Masonic resurgence needs to be a multi-year effort. Serious progress towards that resurgence will require consistent leadership and commitment, not only from any one Grand Master, but also from his successors over the course of decades. Thus, the Grand Master would do well to obtain such commitments from the Deputy Grand Master, the Senior and Junior Grand Wardens, and the Senior and Junior Grand Deacons. Only by consistent efforts across successive Grand Lodge administrations can any Grand Master hope to be effective in helping Freemasonry to resurge.

3. Coordinate efforts throughout the jurisdiction.

The Grand Master can coordinate the efforts of the entire Grand Lodge, and every active Mason therein, by accomplishing three subtasks:

a) The Grand Master can develop initiatives for the Grand Lodge to pursue as an entity, such as a statewide Masonic Day/Grand Lodge Open House, historical reenactments and commemorations, and so forth.

b) The Grand Master can develop initiatives that individual Districts can adapt to their circumstances, such as programs for Masonic Open Houses.

c) The Grand Master can direct that informational materials be prepared and published online, in print, or in both media. Such information has much more weight coming from a Grand Lodge than from an individual.

4. Train District Deputy Grand Masters

The Grand Master can train DDGMs to focus on the tasks of the Masonic resurgence (described in the rest of this book) when, in turn, *they* train lodge leaders and address both leaders and rank-and-file lodge members. A message from the Grand Master delivered by a DDGM can have a powerful effect on a District, its lodges, and its Masons.

5. Instruct and inspire lodge leadership and members

The Grand Master instructs and inspires the line leaders of lodges and rank-and-file Masons directly, through Grand Master Messages published throughout the jurisdiction, District conferences (which Grand Masters often attend as a matter of course) and visits to Particular Lodges (which Grand Masters often do as well). This instruction can focus on one or more of the Five Tasks of the Masonic resurgence.

In sum, the question "who shall bring about the Masonic resurgence?" has a clear answer. The individual Freemason, as well as the lodge's Worshipful Master, the DDGM, and the Grand Master, each have roles and responsibilities to make this resurgence come about. I describe specific actions that each of us can take to further this effort, in the remainder of this book.

8

The First Task: <u>Repair the Temple</u>

Refine the Lodge Experience

You will recall that in Chapter 6 above ("American Freemasonry Today") I identified five major reasons for the Masonic decline. The first of those reasons was that, in many lodges, Masonry is not delivering what it promises—and so men leave Masonry. In this chapter, we directly address this problem.

To create the resurgence of Freemasonry, we must face five great tasks. Because we are a society of symbolic Builders, I describe these tasks in terms of five symbolic structures that we should repair or build outright.

The First Task of the Masonic Resurgence is to "Repair the Temple." By this, I mean that **we must improve the lodge experience, so that it better fulfills the promise that we make to men upon their initiation: the promise that Freemasonry will help them understand more about the great questions of life, and that Masonry will help them become better men.**

If we improve the lodge experience, this alone will largely solve our problems with retention and NPDs. If we do *not* refine the lodge experience, almost nothing else that we do will make a difference as Freemasonry heads toward extinction.

Here are some specific ways to refine the Lodge experience. (I number recommendations sequentially throughout Part Three for ease of reference.

Refine the Stated Communication

Part of the First Task requires us to rethink the way that we conduct the Stated Communication. Right now, in many lodges, the Stated is basically a business meeting—something that neither inspires men to better, more thoughtful lives, nor exerts any influence to keep them coming to lodge. Masonic education, if offered at all, is treated something like a television show's brief commercial message: "And now, a word from our sponsor—Masonic symbolism, philosophy, and history!" We need to turn our priorities right around when it comes to the Stated:

1. **Make Masonic education the heart and soul of the Stated Communication.**

Set aside 20 to, preferably, 30 minutes for Masonic communication in each and every Stated (except when a degree ceremony occurs).[8] Place it early in the meeting to give it the emphasis and time that it deserves. (Please note: this is Recommendation Number One for a reason.)

---

[8]   It may be necessary to abbreviate Masonic education at those Stated Communications when the lodge holds elections or discusses the annual budget. Even then, if at all possible, at least a 10- to 15-minute session of Masonic education should be delivered. At a Stated Communication where the Master Mason Rededication Ceremony is conducted (see below), the entire ceremony is Masonic education. At the official visit of the District Deputy Grand Master, the DDGM's address to the brethren may constitute the Masonic education for the evening.

2. **Do <u>not</u> read out the lodge minutes during the Stated itself.**

Post lodge minutes on a bulletin board for lodge members to read before the *next* Stated. Corrections and approval of the minutes can then proceed in a brief, expeditious manner during the Stated itself.

3. **Do <u>not</u> bring up the payment of budgeted expenses during the Stated.**

When the lodge budget is prepared for the year, as a matter of course, to the greatest extent possible, expenses should be anticipated and specific—with at least a 5% surplus in the budget to handle slight discrepancies in estimation. When the actual expenses occur, if they fall within that 5% overrun or less, their payment should occur without bringing it up to the lodge again. Once a budget including a given expense has been approved, there really is no point to bringing up the payment of that expense again as a matter of lodge business.

4. **Distribute the proposed budget for the upcoming year in writing at least one full Stated Communication before the Stated Communication in which the lodge is to discuss and vote upon the budget.**

This gives the regular attendees of the lodge an opportunity to go over the budget in detail ahead of time, which should streamline the discussion of the budget. One might also send the proposed budget by email to all lodge members, to reduce the chance that someone is first getting an opportunity to see the budget in the meeting where it is being discussed.[9]

Ritual Initiations / Degree Ceremonies

Another part of the First Task involves the way we conduct our ritual initiations.

5. **The Chamber of Reflection should be presented to candidates for at least an hour before each degree.**

This puts candidates in a suitable frame of mind for these solemn ceremonies. (I present a guide to conducting a Chamber of Reflection in Appendix B.)

6. **Distribute each degree's Lecture among <u>several</u> brethren.**

We are blessed to have three magnificent Lectures associated with our degrees. However, there are relatively few brethren who can recite a full degree from memory—and these brethren often are yanked hither, thither, and yon around their Jurisdiction in order to deliver these lectures. In the interest of making each lodge more self-sufficient in presenting their degree work, allow each Lecture to be broken up into (perhaps very small) portions, with multiple brethren each delivering one *portion* of the Lecture from memory.

---

[9]   I realize that not every single lodge member in the United States has an email account. But between email on the one hand, and hardcopy distribution of the budget the Stated before the budget discussion, I would think that almost all the likely attendees at the budget discussion will have had an opportunity to look the proposed budget over in advance of the meeting where it will be discussed.

I realize that this breaks with long-established practice in many Jurisdictions. However, I think we need to come to grips with the fact that in the 21st century, memorization skills are not as emphasized in the educational system as they used to be. Nothing is diminished in the experience by having a Lecture delivered by a succession of brethren instead of one brother—if those brethren are solid in their preparation for their portion.

7. **Do dress rehearsals of the First and Second Degrees, as well as the First Part of the Third Degree (and, if possible, the Second Part)—from memory.**

Full-scale degree rehearsals from memory are a key to presenting a smooth, impressive, and rewarding initiation experience to our Candidates.

The Candidate's Journey Through the Degrees

In most lodges, the Candidate's progress through the degrees is quite rushed, requiring just a month or two to pass before the next degree is conferred. It is not unusual for only two to four months to pass between the day a Candidate is initiated and the day in which that Brother is raised.

How deeply does the initiate ponder the inner truths of Freemasonry between his degree ceremonies when he is experiencing them every month or two? From my own observation and experience, not so much. In many jurisdictions, he simply *can't:* he is busy practicing catechism so that he can present his proficiency and move on to the next degree as soon as possible.

Why do lodges do this? Is it perhaps because there is nothing that their Candidates can do in Freemasonry other than study catechism until they are raised as Master Masons? Is it so that these brothers can be rushed into the officer line? Is it so that these brothers can be hustled into appendant organizations?

The only consideration we should have on our minds here is deepening a brother's experience of Masonic symbolism and philosophy, to the point where we can honestly say that he has begun to change who he is as a person because of what he has received in a degree, before having him progress to the next.

If that means that the lodge has to depend on its longer-tenured Master Masons to fill the officer line, so be it. If that means that the Rites, the Shrine, and so forth languish for membership for a while, so be it. Our objective is to help make men Masons for life. Hence, my following Recommendations.

8. **Slow down a Candidate's progress to allow a thoughtful progression through the degrees.** I suggest an interval of *six months to one* year between *each* degree ceremony that a given Candidate is involved in.

Do not be so shocked at this idea. In the Masonic world at large, this is not a new idea at all. As one Masonic author has pointed out:

> ... it is ... noticeable that membership under a number of other Grand Lodges is expanding, notably in Europe....
>
> Under their system, it takes **up to five years** for a new Apprentice to receive the Master Mason Degree. In the intervening time, the candidate must participate in a great many masonic

education sessions, and is subjected to extensive verbal and written examination prior to his promotion to any higher degree.

[In European Masonry, it] is not easy to attain membership and once attained, promotion takes considerable time and must be earned.... [B]ecause those joining are given significant challenges, these are greatly appreciated and valued when attained. [These are some of the] reasons why **European Masonry is thriving**. (Henderson, 2001, emphases added)

In the spirit of this approach, I have some further Recommendations.

9. **Involve all EAs, FCs,** *and new Master Masons* **in Masonic education during the time of the Stated Communication,** *even if this Masonic education occurs outside of the lodge room.*

Experienced Master Masons appointed by the Worshipful Master can alternate in providing this outside-the-lodge-room Masonic education for the EAs and FCs, so no Master has to miss too much of the Masonic education provided in Stateds conducted on the Third Degree.

I realize that some may find it controversial to have new Master Masons continue in outside-the-lodge-room Masonic Education. However, it is worthwhile to have a new Master Mason receive some orientation in various matters at the very beginning of his tenure as a fully-fledged Mason, before diving into the lodge itself. (Several Grand Lodges consider it important to discuss various aspects of the symbolism and vocabulary presented in the degree, including aspects of the Hiramic legend, as well as a variety of practical aspects of Free-masonry, and other information; see The Most Worshipful Grand Lodge of Free and Accepted Masons of Florida [2008], pp. 18-34, and The Right Worshipful Grand Lodge of Free and Accepted Masons of Pennsylvania [2010], pp. 4-1 through 4-13.)

10. **Masonic education for EAs, FCs, and new MMs should focus on symbolism, philosophy, and history.**

Masonic education for these brethren needs to be much more than just catechism practice sessions. It should involve the exploration of the symbolism and philosophy of the initiations that they have already received. The Lodge System of Education that many Grand Lodges have could be used here (for example, The Most Worshipful Grand Lodge of Free and Accepted Masons of Florida [2018]).[10] In addition, some Grand Lodges include material that could very usefully be discussed with EAs, FCs, and new MMs in materials that they publish for their mentor programs (for example, The Most Worshipful Grand Lodge of Free and Accepted Masons of Florida [2008], and The Right Worshipful Grand Lodge of Free and Accepted Masons of Pennsylvania [2010]).

11. **Each of the Entered Apprentices and Fellowcrafts should be required to accomplish certain tasks during their time between degree ceremonies.**

---

[10]   I have not surveyed all U.S. regular Grand Lodges to see what kind of programs they have. Should anyone need to construct such a program from scratch, he might find it helpful to consult the online resource, Masonic Lodge of Education (2018).

These may include: (a) writing an essay on an aspect of the symbolism of their degree; (b) writing an essay on as aspect of the philosophy of Freemasonry as it is described in their degree; (c) writing an essay on the real-world history of Freemasonry; (d) reciting the full catechism of their degree— perhaps before the full lodge assembled. In the course of six months to (even better) a full year before the next degree, there is plenty of time for the EAs and FCs to both receive instruction in these matters from the Master Masons assigned to work with their class, and to do *all four* of the tasks I have described above. This would truly be proof of their proficiency!

12. **Include EAs or FCs in the full lodge's Masonic education when appropriate.**

When the Masonic education being presented before the full lodge is fully confined to the symbolism or philosophy of the First or Second Degrees, or to real-world Masonic history, lodges may be stepped down to the First or Second Degree to permit the EAs, FCs, and new MMs to attend, as appropriate.

Integrate Brethren into the Life of the Lodge— Thoughtfully

Another part of the First Task involves integrating all brethren into the life of the lodge.

13. **Assign every new Mason to a Masonic Mentor.**

Every new Mason should have an official Mentor for at least his first year or two of membership—after which he should *be* a Mentor. Some Grand Lodges have established formal Mentor development programs, and these should be in more wide use.

I would point out a problem here: *What many Grand Lodges consider "Masonic Mentor programs" are really aspects of Masonic education.* Their programs involve specific lessons on symbolism and so forth. I am talking about a different kind of role all together. The Grand Lodge of Maine, A.F. and A.M., put it well:

> Masonic mentoring is a learning process where a more experienced Brother invests time, energy and Masonic experience in assisting and caring for a new Brother so that he may enjoy and benefit from his Masonry to the full....
>
> **The main thing is to ensure that our newer Brethren are valuing their Masonry so much that they not only wish to stay, but also wish to take an active part, and to recommend membership in the Craft to a friend.** (Grand Lodge of Maine, Ancient Free and Accepted Masons, 2013, pp. 2-3, emphasis in original)

I commend this program to all Grand Lodges and all Particular Lodges.[11] As the then-Grand Master of New York put it, "Take your time and make the new prospect a friend first, and a Mason second! Studies have proven if you make him a true friend, he will never leave our Fraternity!" (Williamson, 2016, p. 5).

14. **Every active Mason should have an ongoing Masonic assignment.**

---

[11] There are other commendable programs, such as that used by the Grand Lodge of New York, but the Maine program is easily available online.

The assignment should reflect both the Mason's individual abilities and interests, on the one hand, and his level of Masonic knowledge and development, on the other. These assignments may involve formal lodge office, to be sure, but most members of the lodge will have other assignments, such as committee member, or specific one-person jobs.

15. Invite inactive lodge members to return to lodge.

Inactive lodge members should receive a signed personal invitation to return, from the officers of the lodge, at least annually, if not more frequently.

16. Use Masonic mentoring to help inactive lodge members to return to lodge.

As the Grand Lodge of Maine notes in their Masonic mentor materials, "Mentoring … may also be used to reactivate … Masons who have stopped attending" (Grand Lodge of Maine, Ancient Free and Accepted Masons, 2013, p. 3).

Hold Special Events

Lodges should hold certain special events.

17. Conduct an annual Master Mason Rededication Ceremony.

One Stated Communication annually should be devoted to a ceremony in which the Master Masons of the lodge symbolically renew the Obligations, and receive the Charges, of the Three Degrees. (This would all be Masonic education.)

Having participated in this ceremony for the first time at Heritage Lodge No. 371 F&AM (GLNY), I can testify to it having a powerful impact on those in attendance. (I present a format for this ceremony in Appendix C.)

18. Hold special presentations by invited lecturers.

Some brethren in other lodges than one's own might be particularly well-informed on some Masonic topics. These brethren might be very happy to present at one's lodge. It is perfectly appropriate to publicize such a presentation on social media so that brethren of other lodges might attend. It is appropriate to offer such brethren an honorarium. On occasion, several lodges may band together to invite a speaker from a distance to a presentation that is either tyled or public.

The Lodge Trestleboard

Finally, the Lodge Trestleboard is often poorly used. Much can be done to make the Trestleboard a vehicle to help brethren have a more meaningful experience with the lodge.

19. Present a symbolic and/or philosophical message in each Lodge Trestleboard.

The three main officers of a lodge have badges of office that represent specific working tools. Each of these working tools has a symbolic significance. It would help members to see a significant message about this symbolism from each of these officers in every issue of the Trestleboard. For example, these officers might quote from a worthwhile Masonic book on their respective themes, *and then apply these ideas to the situation of their specific Lodge today.* These would be worthwhile messages indeed.

Addressing Some Objections

(I address objections to my Recommendations about Masonic education in Chapter 9.)

"Our lodge isn't big enough to do all this! We only have a small number of active members."

Brethren, I do not mean to be flip about this, but if a lodge does *not* implement Recommendations like this, my guess is that it will only get smaller.

One does not require a large lodge to carry out this program. One requires a small number of Masons who are dedicated. If one has enough active Masons in a lodge to open the lodge, plus four (the Tyler, plus one brother each to conduct Masonic education for the EAs, the FCs, and the new MMs), you have enough personnel to carry out everything that I have recommended in this chapter. And, through carrying out these Recommendations—along with Recommendations that I make in subsequent chapters of this book—I expect that your lodge will grow, a lot, and soon.

"If we slow down the progress through the Degrees, Candidates will not stick with Masonry long enough to become Master Masons!"

It is true that popular culture in the West places a strong value on instant gratification. In the face of that, it might seem unlikely that a Candidate might stick with the Fraternity long enough to become a Master Mason if he has to wait six to twelve months between each of his Degree ceremonies.

The weakness of this logic is shown in the assumption that the Candidate will only be *waiting* during these periods. Actually, if my Recommendations are implemented, the Candidate will be extremely busy during the period between his Degree ceremonies. There are (usually) two Stated Communications to attend each month, during which the EAs and FCs each participate in a separate section of Masonic education.

Every once in a while, there will be a Special Communication in which a Degree ceremony is held (since, of course, the EAs, FCs, and new MMs all should attend First Degree ceremonies, and so on.) And between Communications, there are papers to research, topics to study, and catechism to practice, not to mention lodge activities (such as service projects and social functions) to attend.

In short, I don't see many a Candidate dropping out, in the midst of all this activity, unless he simply finds out that Freemasonry and its values are not for him. In that event, it is all the better for us to part ways.

"Our Candidates do not typically have the research and writing skills to do the sorts of tasks you have suggested for EAs, FCs, and new MMs."

This might be so for some candidates in a given lodge. At the least, we can expect variation in these abilities. And certainly, it is very rarely that any Candidate will ever have written a paper on a Masonic topic before.

But this all comes down to a matter of education—*Masonic* education. Early on in the Masonic education given to EAs—perhaps in the very first session—the Instructor should teach EAs what is expected from them in terms of the research papers that they should prepare, and how they should go about preparing them. I have provided guidelines for this in Appendix D.

What "The Four Men of Masonry" Can Do to Further the <u>First</u> Task of the Masonic Resurgence

In Chapter 7, I described "The Four Men of Masonry" as the men who will actually accomplish the resurgence of Freemasonry: the individual Mason, the Worshipful Master, the RW District Deputy Grand Master, and the Most Worshipful Grand Master. Below, I describe what each of these brethren can do to further the First Task of the resurgence, refining the lodge experience.

What the Individual Mason Can Do

There are two general classes of things that the individual, rank-and-file lodge member can do to help further the Masonic resurgence along the lines recommended in this chapter. These categories are *direct action* and *thoughtful Recommendation*.

In terms of direct action, the individual Mason can simply take it upon himself to *do* some of these Recommendations. For example:

- Volunteer to offer a session of Masonic education, and request that you be allowed 20 minutes to do so (see Point #1). (I did this as a relatively new Master Mason, with a very favorable result; see the following section.)

- Volunteer to prepare a Chamber of Reflection before a Degree ceremony (Point #5). Do keep in mind that it will take some time to prepare the materials for a Chamber; you'll need more than a week or two, and you will need to recruit help.

- Assign *yourself* to serve as a Masonic Mentor (even if only unofficially) to a new Mason in your lodge (Recommendation #13).

- Tell the Worshipful Master that you will be glad to fulfill some ongoing Masonic assignment (Point #14). Don't expect office or glory. But know that whatever you are doing, you are supporting your Lodge. In addition, most such responsibilities involve the opportunity to work with other lodge members. Cherish these opportunities.

- As an aspect of the preceding paragraph, note that volunteering to be member of an ad hoc investigation committee is a distinct service to the lodge.

In the "thoughtful Recommendation" department, the individual Mason can further the Masonic resurgence by making an *occasional* Recommendation to the Worshipful Master along the lines of the points mentioned in this chapter. The Masters of lodges are busy men with a challenging responsibility, but they can be receptive to the occasional Recommendation—especially if it comes, not from a kibitzer or critic on the sidelines, but from a Brother who has proven himself by volunteering to provide service in the lodge in other ways.

What the Worshipful Master Can Do

I remember so well the day that the incoming Worshipful Master of my Mother Lodge turned to me, and said that he wanted me to deliver a 20-minute session of Masonic education at *every* Stated Communication (with a few exceptions). In about 30 seconds, the Worshipful Master of my Lodge had instituted an enhanced form of Masonic education.

Such is the power of the Worshipful Master of a Particular Lodge. When it comes to how the Stated Communication works, *within boundaries set by the Grand Lodge*, the WM can simply make it happen. This applies to all my recommendations for the refinement of the Stated Communication (Recommendations #1-#4 above), dress rehearsals (Rec. #7), integrating brethren into the life of the lodge (Recs. #13-#16), special events (Recs. #17-#18), and the Lodge Trestleboard (Rec. #19).

When it comes to my recommendations regarding Degree ceremonies (Recs. #5-#6) and Candidates' journey through the Degrees (Recs. #8-#12), a given Grand Lodge's policies, regulations, or even Masonic Law come into play. It would be extremely wise for a Worshipful Master to at least consult with the District Deputy Grand Master (DDGM) before instituting these changes—and I strongly suggest that the WM do so.

What the District Deputy Grand Master Can Do

The RW District Deputy Grand Master (DDGM) is uniquely situated to bring about change in his Masonic district. The Most Worshipful Grand Master (MWGM) may or may not have the opportunity to visit a given Particular Lodge during his tenure; the DDGM will definitely visit every Particular Lodge in his District, perhaps several times in the course of a year. The DDGM may or may not have a relationship with the Worshipful Master of a given Particular Lodge; the DDGM will know the Worshipful Masters of every Lodge in his District by name and face, and ideally strives to have some kind of personal connection with each. The DDGM is thus an important agent of change in the Masonic resurgence.

The DDGM is in an interesting position in another way, as well. On the one hand, he is the eyes, ears, and hands of the MWGM. As such, it is his responsibility to implement the MWGM's programs and policies, and to report on their progress, success, and observance.

On the other hand, DDGMs also have some opportunity to take initiative on their own. Grand Lodge jurisdictions vary widely in terms of what kind of changes may be made in lodges without Grand Lodge approval. However, I am fairly certain that it would require no special dispensation for a DDGM to make a strong case to the Worshipful Masters in his district that they should make Masonic education the heart and soul of each Stated Communication (Rec. #1).

And so it is for my Recommendations throughout this chapter. For those recommendations that require special consideration by Grand Lodge, the DDGM may well choose to seek such special consideration (such as through a dispensation). For those recommendations that require no such special consideration, the DDGM may simply take it upon himself to recommend that the Particular Lodges in his District institute any given recommendations, made in this chapter, that the DDGM finds of value.

Of course, it is a good idea for the DDGM to let the MWGM know what the DDGM is doing in his District, and what the results are. In turn, this informs the MWGM as he makes his decisions about the direction of the Grand Lodge as a whole.

DDGM Visitations

I have indicated above that the message of the DDGM during his official visit to a lodge may constitute the Masonic Education for the evening. This sets a high standard for the DDGM's message. It is an opportunity for him to inspire the brethren of his district to live better lives as Masons, and to fulfill their Masonic duties, through journey through some selected aspects of Masonic symbolism and philosophy.

Most especially, the DDGM's message at an official visit to a lodge is an opportunity for him to inspire the brethren with a vision of what Freemasonry is and can be. (I hope I may be forgiven for thinking that perhaps some of the material in Part One of this book may be useful to the DDGM in this regard.)

Yes, there will be policy issues to mention to the brethren. However, even these can be framed within a larger vision of furthering the resurgence of Masonry—in the world, and in each Brother's heart.

What the Most Worshipful Grand Master Can Do

The MW Grand Master can make the refinement of the Stated Communication a matter of Grand Lodge policy. It is in his power to institute Recommendations #1-#4 above as standard procedure throughout the Grand Lodge.

The MWGM is uniquely situated to institute jurisdiction-wide policy changes regarding ways in which we work with our Candidates in their initiatory journeys. Whether these changes involve the Chamber of Reflection (Rec. #5), the way in which the Degree Lectures are delivered (Rec. #6), or the weighty issue of the speed with which brethren progress through the degrees (Rec. #8), the MWGM has the power to make changes happen through edicts, directions given through DDGMs, and directions given through messages to the brethren directly. (This is one of those occasions when a monthly MWGM message delivered through a Grand Lodge magazine or newspaper comes in handy; of course, any such message should be reiterated on the Grand Lodge website.)

I have recommended changes in the way that Entered Apprentices, Fellowcrafts, and new Master Masons receive Masonic education (Recs. #9-#12). Here again, the MWGM can institute these changes in a top-down fashion, using (here as elsewhere) DDGMs to both institute these changes and report on their implementation.

The same considerations apply to Recommendations that I have made regarding the thoughtful integration of brethren into the life of their lodge (Recs. #13-#16), the holding of special events (Recs. #17-#18), and the uses of the lodge trestle-board (Rec. #19).

9

The Second Task:
<u>Build the House of Learning</u>

Conduct Quality Masonic Education in the Lodge

Among the five major reasons for the Masonic decline that I identified in Chapter 6 above ("American Freemasonry Today"), the second was that many lodges fail to deliver quality Masonic education. In this chapter, we directly address this problem.

The Second Task of the Masonic resurgence is to Build the House of Learning. By this, I mean that we need to conduct quality Masonic education in the Lodge.[12]

As I mentioned in the preceding chapter, the heart of every Stated Communication should be a substantial period of time devoted to a session of quality Masonic education. In this

---

[12] This chapter presents portions, abbreviated and condensed, from my forthcoming book, *Masonic Education*. The final page of the present book contains ways to connect with my Masonic community, which will be informed of the publication of other Masonic books that I write.

chapter, I explain how to make this sort of Masonic education a regular feature of one's Lodge life. Specifically, I describe:

- what "quality" in Masonic education means;

- how to plan out Masonic education for a lodge;

- how to prepare Masonic education;

- how to present Masonic education.

Let me expand on these four topics a bit. As it happens, I have spent years as a professional educator, teaching at public and private educational institutions including community colleges, four-year colleges, and universities.[13] I have a sense of what sorts of educational experiences make a difference in the lives of students, and what sorts do not. Looking at a lot of what is presented as Masonic education through these lenses, I see that from the outset we need to get some principles straight.

For education to have an impact, it must have the following qualities:

- The overall educational program must have an *objective*. That is, it must be directed to have some specific outcome.

- The overall educational program must present individual lessons or discussion sections in a *logical progression* of material.

---

[13] I had what seems to be the unique experience of being raised as a new Master Mason by one of my own former university students. Thank you, Bro. Jorge.

- Each lesson/discussion must be prepared to meet some *specific objective* that furthers the objective of the overall educational program.

- Each lesson/discussion must be presented in a way that engages the participants, conveys the necessary information, and helps the participants see the *relevance* of the information and how to apply it in their lives.

What is "Quality" in Masonic Education?

In some lodges, the attitude seems to be that the period of Masonic education is really just entertainment presented by means of information. In the television industry, they call this "infotainment."

In many other lodges, what is presented may be categorized as "interesting stuff." These may be incidents from Masonic history, or items of Masonic symbolism or philosophy, presented in a purely informational way. That is, facts are presented, but there is no discussion of the relevance of these facts for the brethren, or the application of these philosophical principles in their lives. In sum, there is no "take-home message" for the brethren.

Quality Masonic education is neither infotainment nor just interesting stuff. Masonry has a point, an objective. Like Masonry itself, every session of Masonic education needs to have the same point and objective, which is as follows:

> **The prime objective of Freemasonry is to further the moral and spiritual perfection of individual Masons, and thereby to advance the moral and spiritual perfection of humanity.[14]**
>
> **The prime objective of Masonic education should be exactly the same.**

Yes, that is quite an agenda. But that is the reality of Freemasonry. We are not a three-century-old dining fraternity. We are not primarily a charitable organization, either. We do emphasize fellowship and charitable works along the way, but Masonry is first and foremost a fraternity intent on personal and societal transformation—and that needs to be our focus in Masonic education, as well. We shall return to this theme.

For now, the important thing to keep in mind is that quality Masonic education—really, the only kind of Masonic education that is worthy of the name—focuses on personal transformation, on the moral and spiritual development of the very brethren in attendance. That is its objective. Everything else in this chapter has that objective in mind.

---

[14]   I realize that this is a powerful statement. I believe that the truth of this assertion is borne out in the teachings conveyed in our ritual and the teachings of major Masonic thinkers over the last three centuries. I hope to expand on this in forthcoming books, particularly *The Mission of Masonry*.

How to Plan Out Masonic Education for a Lodge

In many of those Lodges that do feature Masonic education at all, what are presented are a collection of miscellaneous topics. In one meeting, the brethren hear about the life of a famous Masonic baseball player. At another meeting, there is a presentation on the meaning of some symbol. There may be lessons on topics that are not, strictly speaking, Masonic at all: a session on financial planning, or leadership methods.

If we take seriously the objective of Masonic education as personal transformation, we need to take a different approach here. The sum of your Masonic education sessions over the course of the Masonic year comprises the main part of your Lodge's educational program. As I mentioned earlier, a quality overall educational program must present individual lessons or discussion sections in a logical progression of material. My first Recommendation for this chapter is thus:

20. **Each incoming Master of the Lodge should lead the planning of a curriculum for the Masonic education for his year.**

This planning entails several tasks, described below.

a. **Determine the dates on which Masonic education will be delivered in the Lodge.**

Much as I hate to say it, it may not be practical to deliver Masonic education on the dates when Grand Lodge officials visit the lodge. In addition, some lodges hold degree ceremonies on Stated Communications, and at those meetings the degree work itself constitutes the Masonic education. Determining what dates are available for Masonic education makes clear exactly how much one can cover in the course of the Master's year.

b. Determine the *overall* area or areas to address in Masonic education this year.

The Master's basic choices here are (1) Masonic philosophy, (2) Masonic symbolism (3) Masonic history (including local Masonic history, and biographies of prominent Masons); and (4) the Lodge System of Instruction (name varies) published by the Grand Lodge. Some Masters will want to pick one area for the year. In those Lodges which meet twice monthly, some Masters will like to have one area addressed at the first meeting, and another addressed at the second meeting, all year through. Yet other Masters will take an alternating approach of all these overall areas (one meeting on philosophy, one meeting on symbolism, etc.; rinse and repeat). Some Masters will take the 'Chinese menu' approach (for example, four sessions in a row of philosophy, followed by four of symbolism, and so on).

How does the Master make the choice? By considering the circumstances of the brethren of his Lodge. This would be a good subject of personal meditation. What does this Lodge most need to hear this year? (Frankly, if one is choosing amongst Masonic philosophy, symbolism, and history, and the Lodge System of Instruction, one can hardly go wrong.)

c. Determine the *specific* topics to address in *each* session of Masonic education this year.

This is actually less daunting than it may seem.

In terms of Masonic <u>philosophy</u>, one cannot go wrong with:

a) the principles that are *explicitly* named during our degree ceremonies, including the degree lectures (such as the three principle tenets of our profession; the three theological virtues; the three great supports of Masonry; the four cardinal virtues); and,

b) the principles that are *implicit* in our degree ceremonies and practices (the fatherhood of God and the brotherhood of man; the equality of men in the lodge; our attitude towards the VSL; freedom of religious and political belief; Masonry as joining spiritual faith, on the one hand, with reason and science, on the other).

In terms of Masonic <u>symbolism</u> (which of course will involve the philosophical principles behind our symbols), one may choose from the wealth of the working tools, the Monitorial symbols, and the other symbols observable in the lodge and degree ceremonies (some being subtle in nature).

In terms of Masonic <u>history</u>, there are a wealth of events in international, national, regional, and even Particular Lodge history that one might choose.

d. Determine who will teach these sessions of Masonic education.

Some Masters will want to teach some—or even all—of the Masonic education sessions themselves. Some will want to assign one particular brother to handle all of them. Some will want multiple instructors. All of this is up to the circumstances of the individual Lodge.

What is crucially important here is that instructors are assigned in advance, with enough time to prepare. In my experience, it pays to have each instructor assigned at the very least one full month in advance of his lesson—longer, if a holiday or vacation period fall in the month before the lesson. And it is a very good idea for the WM or another assigned officer to look in on the instructor periodically, to see how their lesson preparation is coming along.

When an instructor is assigned, the WM or his assign should specify the following: (1) the topic, (2) how much time is allotted for discussion of this topic in the meeting, and (3) the imperative to focus on the personal relevance and implementation of principles discussed—all in the interest of personal transformation.

How to <u>Prepare</u> Masonic Education

(I address myself in this section to individuals who have been assigned to deliver one or more sessions of Masonic education as an instructor.)

I have advocated above that it is actually the Worshipful Master of the Lodge who should select your topic. However, I realize that in practice many WMs will leave that choice up to you, the instructor. In this case, read what I have written above about selecting topics (Recommendation #20c).

My second major Recommendation for this chapter is:

21. **Instructors should devote significant time in study, composition, and practice for <u>each</u> session of Masonic education.**

You should plan on spending significant time in the preparation of a session of Masonic education, especially when you are starting out. We are talking hours, not minutes, per session. You should look at your presentation in terms of three stages: study, composition, and practice. I address each of these below.

Preparation Stage #1: Study

Do not kid yourself here. I do not care how much experience you have as a Freemason, how much ritual you have memorized, how many degree Lectures you have down pat, or what sorts of awards you may have for your Masonic knowledge.

If you are going to presume to instruct your brethren about Freemasonry, you should study about your topic anew in order to prepare your lesson. There will be something new for you to learn, almost certainly. And it may well be the case that something will occur to you as you study that is particularly relevant to the current circumstances of your Lodge that you will wish to emphasize in your lesson.

Preparation Stage #2: Structuring Your Lesson

Here is a format that you can use to structure your lesson. Each bullet point below becomes a heading in your lesson.

- Title of the Lesson
- Date, Time, and Venue
- Objective
- Introduction
- Major Points

- Conclusion

Title, date, time, and venue are self-explanatory. I address the other parts of your lesson structure below.

Objective

This may be Recommendation #22, but it is the First Commandment of quality Masonic education:

22. **Instructors should always have a moral point as part of their lesson objectives.**

As I mention above, Masonic education is not just about conveying information. Ultimately, Masonic education is about helping brethren with their personal transformation into better human beings, so that we can better society. (If that sounds a bit "cosmic," well, that's Freemasonry.) Given that this is the purpose of Masonic education, you should always have a moral point as part of your lesson objectives.

I always write out a lesson objective whenever I teach. The following are good examples of lesson objectives:

- (for a lesson on Masonic philosophy:) By the conclusion of this lesson, Lodge members will understand:

    a) where and when the philosophical principle of __ first showed up in the wisdom literature during human history;

    b) the meaning of this principle; and,

    c) how to apply this principle in their personal lives, and in their relationships with their families, co-workers or co-students, members of their community, and/or other lodge members.

- (for a lesson on Masonic symbolism:) By the conclusion of this lesson, Lodge members will understand the following about the meaning of the symbol __:

  a) he *Surface* level (such as, "the _ is a tool used by operative Mason to ...," or "this symbol depicts a _, which in ordinary life is ...");

  b) the *Moral* level (such as, "but we, as Masons, use the _ to ...," or "this is an emblem of ...";

  c) the *Behavioral* level (how the principle mentioned in the Moral level might actually apply in the daily life of the Mason); and,

  d) the *Esoteric* level (what the symbol teaches us about the universe, the spiritual world, and/or the nature of reality itself).

- (for a lesson on Masonic history:) By the conclusion of this lesson, Lodge members will understand the following about the historical event __:

  a) what happened, where, when, why, and who was involved;

  b) what moral lessons can be drawn from this event;

  c) the implications of these moral lessons for the brethren's personal lives, and for their relationships with their families, co-workers or co-students, members of their community, and/or other lodge members.

Introduction

Many years ago, a supervisor taught me a style of structuring a speech that he had learned in the U.S. Army: "Tell them what you are *going* to tell them. Then *tell* them. Then tell them what you *told* them." It was not until years later that I learned that this was essentially the advice of the great philosopher Aristotle, the tutor of Alexander the Great himself. I try to use this advice in all my presentations, and I think it is good advice for you, as well.

Your Introduction might be very short: "Tonight I will present to you my thoughts on an important <principle of Masonic philosophy> <aspect of Masonic symbolism> <event in Masonic history>." If you choose this topic yourself, you might wish to explain *why* you chose it. If you have some special connection to this topic, if it means something special to you personally, it would be appropriate to express that, perhaps in a brief anecdote, in the Introduction (or Conclusion).

But—and I am begging here—do **_not_** begin with either a long baseball-style wind-up or a joke.

I have seen a brother waste five minutes of a lesson in unnecessary introductory material, explaining how the Senior Warden asked him to give the lesson, and at first he said no, and then he said yes, but then he didn't know where to look up information on the topic, and then …. When I hear such things, I am screaming inside. So will your audience.

Similarly, I have rarely seen humor used well in Masonic education. I do know that many brothers have been taught to use a joke "as an icebreaker." Let me tell you about icebreakers.

If you are presenting a session of Masonic education, you are addressing a group of brethren, each of whom has invested hours of his life receiving his own Masonic degrees. As a group, they have just been through perhaps half an hour of the ritual of the opening of the Lodge, and perhaps other Lodge business. Trust me: *the ice has already been broken by the time you stand up to speak!* Now what they want is education, not comedy.

If you are addressing 30 brethren in a Lodge meeting, then every two minutes that the instructor wastes translates into an hour of collective human life lost. Life is short enough; let us use our time productively.

Major Points

Once the Objectives are set down, the Major Points of the lesson almost write themselves. Simply address your Objectives, point by point, and you will have a very good lesson.

Conclusion

No lesson should just come to a sudden end, like a car disappearing from sight over a cliff. There should always be some words of conclusion. You could summarize your main points, reiterating them in short form. You could reemphasize the implications that your presentation has for the lives of the Masons present.

Always thank the Worshipful Master and Wardens for the opportunity to present your thoughts to the Lodge. Always thank the brethren assembled for their attention. None of this is wasted time. My personal favorite last line in a presentation: "Thank you for your kind attention."

Writing/Printing Out Your Lesson

Even though I deliver my lessons looking at the brethren in the audience, I still write or type my lesson to accomplish three things: (1) fix the material in my mind, (2) provide something to help me review the material on the day I will deliver the lesson, and (3) provide something for me to refer back to when I am in the midst of delivering the lesson. Underline words that you know you will want to emphasize.

I often print out two copies of the talk from a computer file: one in regular-sized type from which I can make copies to give to brethren who express interest, and one in a very large font (say, 20-point or larger font) to look at when I am actually delivering the lesson in lodge.

Preparation Stage #3: Practice

Always, always, always practice your presentation before you give it. I like to read out my talks three times before I present them:

- First, I read it out loud to myself. I always find material I want to change, often quite a lot of material, and so I make a bunch of changes.

- Second, I read it out loud to myself to check for time. **You must know how long your talk takes to deliver.** I will be saying more about this in a little bit. (I've been known to make changes here, too.)

- Third, I like to read it out loud to an audience. If I can get a Masonic friend to listen to me, even over the phone, I find that the experience and the feedback can be very useful. (I also usually make changes at this stage, too.)

Concerning time, this is the Second Commandment of quality Masonic education:

23. **Always deliver your presentation within the time allotted. Do not go overtime. Do not end early.**

If the Worshipful Master said I should take 20 minutes for the presentation, my presentation will take between 19 minutes and 20 minutes. If he said I should take 10 minutes, but I could go a little longer if I really need to, my presentation will take between 9 and 10 minutes on the dot. (Who can tell whether *my* sense of whether I really need to go longer coincides with *his?*)

The Master of the Lodge is, well, the Master of the Lodge's meeting, as well. You will follow the directions given by him and his assigns for your presentation.

How to <u>Present</u> Masonic Education

Here is the Third Commandment of quality Masonic education:

24. **Follow best practices for making oral presentations when you deliver your lesson before the Lodge.**

I have heard that a research study found that a significant number of people fear public speaking more than death itself.

Presenting a session of Masonic education does not have to be a terrifying experience. Here are a few tips to make the experience not just survivable, but enjoyable for all involved. The tips are divided into Internal Issues—things that the instructor should keep in mind—and External Issues—things that the instructor should do, or not do.

Internal Issues

A lesson is not a speech.

A session or lesson of Masonic education is not like a formal speech. The lesson can (and really should) have a conversational tone, and it does not have to be delivered word-perfectly.

Everyone is on your side here.

No one is forcing anyone to attend your lesson; everyone is there voluntarily. They *want* you to succeed. And a Lodge can be a very forgiving audience; if you lose your place and have to check notes, no one is going to boo or throw tomatoes at you. After all, you're the brother who had the initiative to get up and give a lesson. You are providing service to them, and they know it.

External Issues

Eye contact is key.

When I make a presentation in Lodge, I make it a point to look from face to face throughout the room. I do not mean just look up from your notes once in a while. I may gesture to a specific individual for emphasis. Eye contact increases attention and personal investment on the part of the audience.

Of course, that means you have to know your material. When I present, I usually use a music stand or podium to hold my notes, as a backup, but most of the time I am looking at my audience.

Stand (and walk) among your brethren.

At most of my lesson presentations, I do not present from the East (a location that I reserve for presenting a formal research paper). For lessons, I prefer to present from the floor of the lodge, standing on the same level (or even a little lower) than the brethren who comprise my audience. I walk around, directing myself at one moment to the brethren sitting in the southeast, at another to those in the southwest or the north, and sometimes right to the Senior Warden in the West, just to keep him upright in his chair. (People do not usually snooze during my lessons, partly for this reason.)

Use the Lodge itself as one big visual aid.

The Lodge itself is a collection of symbols. When I need to re-enact a small portion of the ritual to make a point—well, the location of that very ritual is where I am delivering the lesson! I do take care *not* to cross the line of sight between the Worshipful Master and the Volume of Sacred Law on the Altar, but otherwise I make full use of the space of the Lodge.

Are you making reference to a symbol? Perhaps it is on a jewel or apron that one of the officers wears: point to it. (Some lodges have a collection of the working tools set up in a display in the Eastern side of the lodge; I'll use that, too.) Because so many lessons involve self-improvement, I will point to the Ashlars, which are often in the East as well. The Altar, the Great Lights in Masonry—all are fair to make reference to, say, by pointing at close range.

Be interactive.

If you make a reference to the text of the ritual, start the phrase but ask the brethren to complete it. Ask a question from the catechism and look for a response from the group. And I almost *never* answer these questions for them. (I have been known to say, "brethren, I know you know this; it's going to be an awfully long night here if I don't hear from you.")

Use the Lodge's time well.

Be ever mindful that you have the rare opportunity of being the full focus of attention of a group of people who are seeking personal enlightenment. Use their time well.

Addressing Some Objections

"The Lodge members will not sit still for 20 to 30 minutes of Masonic education!"

This is simply not credible. If someone can pay attention to a game in the Super Bowl, the World Series, or the World Cup, then he can pay attention to 20 to 30 minutes of Masonic education.

Now, this Masonic education needs to be engaging, thought provoking, and worthwhile. I have addressed these issues throughout this chapter.

"Our brethren are not prepared to teach a lesson of 20 to 30 minutes in length."

If someone can survive writing a passing paper for a high school class, he has the basic cognitive equipment to teach a lesson of 20 to 30 minutes in length. What many of our brethren lack is a knowledge of how to approach the task. Here, too, I have addressed this issue throughout this chapter.

"But our brethren are not professional educators! Nor are they prepared to teach with the objective of bringing about 'personal transformation'!"

Your brethren are probably not professional actors, either, and yet they act out the Hiramic drama. Few of them are professional managers, but they nonetheless run their Lodge.

In Freemasonry, we use the talent available. Educating is about using certain principles that motivated brethren can learn; I have mentioned some of them above (and I go into more detail in my forthcoming book *Masonic Education*).

Personal transformation is the product of experiences (like our initiation ceremonies) and teaching about one's moral and spiritual improvement (which is what Masonic education is supposed to be all about). The term "personal transformation" may sound all transcendent and downright cosmic, but this is what Freemasonry itself has been about for over 300 years; the only problem is that many of us seem to have forgotten this. Teach (and live) the lessons of Masonic philosophy, Masonic symbolism, even Masonic history; back this up with the experiential learning that is possible through Masonic ritual; personal transformation will occur.

What "The Four Men of Masonry" Can Do to Further the <u>Second</u> Task of the Masonic Resurgence

What the Individual Mason Can Do

The individual Mason can do several things to further the Second Task of the Masonic Resurgence.

<u>First, the individual Mason can *volunteer* to teach a session of Masonic education—the way it ought to be taught.</u> There is no better way to demonstrate the value of quality Masonic education than by actually *delivering* some. Do that, and some wonderful things can happen.

That's what happened in my lodge.

I was a fairly newly minted Mason when I volunteered to deliver a session or two of Masonic education. (I looked at it as a Masonic responsibility.) Like many Lodges, my mother Lodge had Masonic education now and then, without an overall plan, when brethren volunteered to present something of interest to them.

When the Master agreed to my request, I prepared a lesson in the same way I had presented lessons for years, from adult Sunday School to the university classroom: as part of an overall approach to the subject (which for me was now Masonic symbolism), always with objectives in mind, including a behavioral objective. When I presented, I presented as I recommended above: lots of eye contact, using the Lodge room itself. The brethren seemed to like the lessons.

Then a funny thing happened.

At the following Installation of Officers, I was appointed the Marshall—in this lodge, the absolutely lowest-ranked officer. Soon after the installation, the new Master—who had watched my lessons as the former Senior Warden—said two sentences to me:

"Mark, I want you to teach Masonic education at every Stated. And I want you to teach it for 20 minutes."

And just like that >*BAM*< Winter Park Lodge #239 in Florida had Masonic education at every one of its Stated Communications.

The power of a volunteer stepping out on a limb: It's a thing.

Second, the individual Mason (preferably with several others) can approach the Worshipful Master of the Lodge and ask for quality Masonic education to occur as a prominent and regular component of the Stated Communication.

The typical Worshipful Master wants to give his Lodge's brethren what they want in terms of a Masonic experience. If a Mason—with the backing of, say, five or ten other members of the Lodge—approach the Worshipful Master with the idea of introducing quality, regular Masonic education, it is the rare Worshipful Master who would not at least throw that before the Lodge for discussion.

This is all very important. **Helping to deliver quality Masonic education in your Lodge is the single action most likely to reduce the number of NPDs from your Lodge.** The importance of this act cannot be overestimated.

What the Worshipful Master Can Do

This is where the rubber really meets the road. As is clear from my own experience being appointed to deliver Masonic education, the Worshipful Master can make regular Masonic education in the Lodge happen, in a matter of seconds, by fiat, period, full stop.

Now, in order to have a *quality* experience in the Lodge, the Worshipful Master will need to go farther. He should lay out a curriculum for the designated instructor to follow (as I describe earlier in this chapter). He should even instruct the designated instructor in how to prepare and deliver Masonic education (all of which I describe earlier in this chapter). But this instruction need not take a very long time; with a minimal investment of effort, your Lodge could have quality Masonic education for some time to come. (The wise Worshipful Master will involve his Wardens in fixing the curriculum, and in instructing the instructors, to help ensure continuity in Masonic education over time.)

As I have said, this is very important. **Instituting regular quality Masonic education in your Lodge is the single action most likely to reduce the number of NPDs from your Lodge.** The importance of this act cannot be overestimated.

What the District Deputy Grand Master Can Do

With the approval of the MW Grand Master himself, the RW DDGM can institute quality Masonic education throughout his District.

The DDGM will almost certainly need to instruct the Worshipful Masters in how to structure a curriculum, and in how to instruct instructors regarding the preparation and delivery quality Masonic education. That can be done in a single, well-planned meeting, attended by the Worshipful Masters and (I would hope) the Senior and Junior Wardens of the District. (Many Grand Lodges have a District-level Masters and Wardens Meeting at regular intervals; this sounds like a good topic for such a meeting.)

After the initial instruction, then it becomes a matter of measuring compliance. This fits in perfectly with the DDGM's general responsibilities.

Once again, this is very important. **Instituting regular quality Masonic education at each Lodge in your District is the single action most likely to reduce the number of NPDs in your District.** The importance of this act cannot be overestimated.

What the Most Worshipful Grand Master Can Do

What I wrote earlier about the power of the Worshipful Master to institute Masonic education in his Lodge by fiat applies on a much larger scale to the Most Worshipful Grand Master. One Edict, and regular Masonic education is instituted throughout the Jurisdiction.

What might one say in such an Edict? Consider these possibilities:

- Every Lodge should have a session of Masonic education at every Stated Communication, with certain specific exceptions. These exceptions would include degree work, installations, and perhaps elections. (I would tend to have Masonic education even during the official visit of a Grand Lodge officer, but not all will agree.)

- This Masonic education should take 20-30 minutes of the Stated Communication.

- Within any Particular Lodge, the curriculum for this Masonic education should be based on a consideration of Masonic philosophy, Masonic symbolism, Masonic history, and/or the Grand Lodge System of Education.

- The Worshipful Master of each Particular Lodge should determine the curriculum for his Lodge.

- Each session of Masonic education should include a substantial focus on improving the moral or spiritual dimensions of the Brother's life, by focusing on his external or internal behavior.

This is about as much as can be accomplished by fiat. Beyond an Edict, the Grand Master or his direct assign should teach the DDGMs in how to teach Worshipful Masters of Lodges in how to set a curriculum, and how to instruct their Lodge instructors in how to prepare and teach sessions of Masonic education. In addition, the Grand Master or his direct assign needs to instruct the DDGMs that monitoring compliance with this Edict or policy is an integral part of their official responsibilities.

As I have mentioned before, this is very important. **Instituting regular quality Masonic education at each Lodge in your Grand Jurisdiction is the single action most likely to reduce the number of NPDs in your Grand Lodge.** The importance of this act cannot be overestimated.

10

The Third Task: <u>Build the Lighthouse</u>

Tell the World About Freemasonry

Among the five major reasons for the Masonic decline that I identified in Chapter 6 above ("American Freemasonry Today"), the third was that very few people in general society have an accurate idea about Freemasonry—or even know that it still exists. In this chapter, we directly address this problem.

The Third Task of the Masonic resurgence is to Build the Lighthouse. By this, I mean that we should tell the world about Freemasonry.

As things stand today, most of the public either does not even know that Freemasonry still exists, or they have inaccurate—even bizarre—notions about who we are and what we do. In this context, telling the public that we exist, who we really are, and what we stand for, is not only *not* a violation of Masonic ethics—it is *necessary to fulfill* the purposes of Freemasonry (concerning which, see Chapter 4).

Below, I give some recommendations for accomplishing the Third Task.

Tell the World Face to Face

People are most inclined to believe what they actually see and directly experience. Masons should use the vehicle of the Open House to give people from the general public the experience of meeting Masons and hearing us explain what we are about.

25. **Each Particular Lodge should hold an Open House for the public, *annually*.**

Lodges that share a building may opt to hold one joint Open House. Lodges that are very small might find it useful to have assistance from the brethren of another nearby lodge.

In a Particular Lodge Open House, the objectives of an Open House are quite straightforward. We want the public to understand five things about Freemasonry—the Five Messages of the Masonic Open House:

a) The Masonic Fraternity not only still exists, but it meets in their community.

b) Freemasonry is a fraternal society of adult men who are interested in improving their characters through symbolic and philosophical initiations and discussions.

c) Freemasonry has nothing to do with the many rumors that people hear: Masonry is not a religion; Masonry is not concerned with world domination, mind control, or devil worship.

d) There is a process that men can follow if they would like to become Freemasons.

e) There are local organizations affiliated with Freemasonry for women and for youth.

That's it. These messages are not hard to convey. Any lodge that can pull together about ten brethren to carry out the event can convey these messages successfully.

The event does have a few moving parts, as it were. I describe how to put together a Masonic Open House in Appendix E.

26. Particular Lodges should take care to adequately publicize the Open House in advance.

There is no point to even holding an Open House if people do not know about it in advance! A Lodge should do the following, in order to publicize their event:

- Print up handbills for the brethren of the lodge to pass out to their friends and neighbors. The handbill would say something like "Masonic Lodge Open House — Learn About the Freemasons — <date and time of the event> — <Name and address of the lodge> — Families welcome."

- Make a large sign to post on the street or the roadside near the Lodge. It would give the text of the handbill.

- Lodge finances allowing, it would be good to place a quarter-page or one-eighth-page advertisement in a local newspaper. The text of the ad could be like the handbill.

- Again, Lodge finances allowing, it would be good to have posters professionally printed, of the type that advertise entertainment, church, or recreational events. These posters would then be placed in shop windows in the community a week or two before the event.

- It would be good to have a chat with reporters from a local newspaper, local radio stations, and local television stations. There are two purposes for these interviews: one, to get advance publicity for the Open House (which could increase attendance), and two, to get coverage of the event itself (which increases public awareness of the Fraternity). Note that newspaper reporters need a lot of advance notice if the hope is that they will print something in advance of the event itself.

Now for some recommendations at the District and Grand Lodge level.

27. The Particular Lodges within a given District might all hold Masonic Open Houses on the same day.

There are several advantages to holding Open Houses on the same day within a given District. Blanketing the area of the District with Masonic publicity will raise awareness that Freemasonry still exists throughout the entire District. People out driving or walking may see signs publicizing several different lodges' Open Houses during a single drive or walk; this may lead to sufficient curiosity to encourage attendance at one of them. If there is radio or television coverage throughout an area, this might prompt people to attend the Open House of a closer lodge that was not itself the subject of the TV or radio interviews.

28. Alternatively, the Particular Lodges within a given District may hold Masonic Open Houses at different dates carefully distributed throughout the calendar year.

There are advantages to this approach as well. Holding Open Houses throughout the calendar year may make it possible for people to attend at some point whose work or personal schedule makes it impossible for them to attend during some given District Masonic Day.

29. Grand Lodge should hold a Masonic Day at Grand Lodge headquarters annually. This is essentially like a Particular Lodge's Open House, but conducted on a larger scale.

Masonic Day at the Grand Lodge can be an altogether grander affair than what any Particular Lodge can put on. Many Grand Lodges have libraries, large meeting rooms, and sumptuously appointed conference rooms. In addition, there are sometimes multiple lodge rooms within the Grand Lodge headquarters building, rooms that can be pressed into service for Masonic Day.

It is important to note that the Grand Lodge Masonic Day has the same objectives, and the same Five Messages, as a Particular Lodge Open House. What is different is that, first, the Grand Lodge typically has a physical setting that is more impressive for outsiders, and second, the Grand Lodge can attract a higher level of media coverage than the typical Particular Lodge.

There are a few more moving parts to a Grand Lodge Masonic Day than to a Particular Lodge Open House. I address the nuts and bolts of these in Appendix E, as well.

30. Open the annual installation of Particular Lodge officers to family and friends of lodge members.

I attended an installation just last night, as I write these words in June 2018. For the three close family members of one of the new officers, it was the first Masonic function they had ever attended. I am sure that seeing the Bible on the altar, and hearing the prayers of the Chaplain, put any lingering doubts about the positive character of Freemasonry to rest in their minds, and in the minds of any of the other non-Masonic friends of lodge members visiting the installation of the officers of Joshua Lodge #890 F&AM (GLNY).

I know for a fact that when I was installed as Marshall at Winter Park Lodge #239 F&AM (GLFL), many of those in attendance were friends of lodge members, many of whom had never seen the inside of a lodge before. The installation made a very positive impression on them.

The lodge installation is also an opportunity to invite local media. For example, local newspapers are always on the lookout for colorful local stories, and lodge installations in appropriate regalia are nothing if not that.

Tell the World Online

There is a limit on the number of people with whom one can meet face to face at any given time. There is, for all practical purposes, no limit to the number of people with whom one can "meet" online, at any given time. Both Grand Lodges and Particular Lodges can carry out some low-cost or no-cost activities to heighten the profile of Freemasonry in a responsible way in their communities, the nation as a whole, and the world at large.

These activities involve websites and online video. I address each of these areas separately below.

Websites

I have recommendations for both Grand Lodges and Particular Lodges concerning their websites.

31. The Grand Lodge website should have a special section specifically for non-Masons who are interested in learning about the Fraternity.

On the Grand Lodge website's homepage, let one of the tabs be labeled "For Non-Masons." Let us openly and explicitly address this huge population, the group that includes every Petitioner we shall ever have.

The "For Non-Masons" tab leads to a sort of website-within-a-website on the Grand Lodge site. The "For Non-Masons" page should have a welcoming message for the non-Mason, and should have links to at least the following pages:

- **What Freemasonry Is**: At the very least, set out the Five Messages of the Masonic Open House, which I described earlier in this chapter. To go farther, this would be a good place to describe some Masonic values and philosophy, how Masonry began, and how Freemasonry is organized (that is, with a sovereign Grand Lodge within every U.S. state, Puerto Rico, and DC, with Particular Lodges in many communities).

- **What Freemasonry Is Not**: Explicitly address some of the major myths about the Fraternity. Explain that we are not a religion, we are not a conspiracy to rule the world, we are not involved in devil worship, and we do not determine the winners of either the World Series, the Super Bowl, the Academy Awards, or political elections.

- **How to Become a Freemason**: Describe the process in your grand jurisdiction.

- **Locate a Lodge**: See the next numbered recommendation below for how to arrange this section.

- **Frequently Asked Questions About Freemasonry** (abbreviated as "FAQs" in the navigation bar): This is the place to answer, in one place, a selection of those many questions that so many people have about Freemasonry. These include questions like, "Why do Freemasons wear aprons?", "Can women become Freemasons?", "Is Freemasonry occult?", "Can Christians become Freemasons?", "What does the Masonic symbol [note: the Square and Compasses] mean?", and so forth, and so on.

- **Resources for Further Study**: This would be the place to list responsible and accurate resources for further study about basic truths regarding Freemasonry, both in print and online, for non-Masons. Online resources would include:

  - ➢ **Website of the Grand Lodge of British Columbia and Yukon** (link to http://freemasonry.bcy.ca/sitemap.html): This site has over 3,800 pages of well-researched articles.

> ➤ **A Page About Freemasonry** (link to http://web.mit.edu/dryfoo/Masons/): by RW Gary L. Dryfoos, established in 1994.

> ➤ **Anti-Masonry Points of View** (link to http://www.masonicinfo.com/): by W. Bro. Edward L. King, established in 1998; includes many articles refuting anti-Masonic charges, as well as other general information about the Fraternity.

When it comes to print resources, it is important to emphasize material that is appropriate for the modern non-Mason. This is *not* the place for deep, philosophically or mystically oriented treatises, nor for a lot of flowery 19th century English. I would include the following three books (including respective links to Amazon):

> ➤ *Freemasonry: An Introduction*, by Mark Koltko-Rivera.

> ➤ *Freemasons for Dummies*, by Christopher Hodapp.

> ➤ *The Complete Idiot's Guide to Freemasonry*, by S. Brent Morris.

- **(optional) The History of Freemasonry**: For Grand Lodges that wish to go into detail, it might be wise to have a separate page for this topic, rather than to address it at length on the "What Freemasonry Is" page. This optional page would also be the place to describe your own Grand Lodge history.

32. The Grand Lodge website "For Non-Masons" section should list lodges alphabetically *by the communities they are located in.*

Grand Lodge websites tend to be developed to appeal to other Masons, not the curious non-Mason. This needs to change if we are to further the resurgence of Freemasonry. Nowhere is this clearer than the listing of lodges.

The non-Mason has no particular interest in the sequential numbers of lodges. He does not even know what a Masonic district is, nor does it matter to him that Solomon's Lodge #987 is in the Third Masonic District. Nor are the names of lodges especially meaningful to him. And yet, typically, what he finds on the Grand Lodge website is a sequential list of lodges by number, listing each lodge's name and Masonic district. The list *might* include a town, but at best this arrangement requires the non-Mason to search through listings of dozens or hundreds of lodges, trying to find one near him.

When it comes to lodge information, what is important to a non-Mason curious about Freemasonry is finding out two things: where his local lodge is, and how he can contact them. Consequently, he needs to see a listing on the website like the following:

Location	Lodge	Interested parties
Arcadia	Hiram Lodge #278	Contact our lodge secretary by email sent to secretary@hiram278.com, or by mail sent to PO Box 99, Arcadia <ZIP code>
Avalon	Solomon's Lodge #987	Contact our lodge secretary by email sent to secretary@sol970.com, or by mail sent to PO Box 76, Avalon <State and ZIP code>. Feel free to attend our open dinner on the second Tuesday of every month at 7:30 p.m., at the lodge building, 33 Temple Lane, in western Avalon.

What this means is that the Grand Lodge website needs to have *two* listings of lodges: one in the section for Masons (which will list lodges alphabetically,[15] and include things like the Masonic district), and one in the section for non-Masons, which has a listing such as I have shown above.

---

[15] Even for Masons, it is useless to list lodges in order of number, a practice which serves no purpose other than to make low-numbered lodges feel prestigious.

33. Every Particular Lodge should develop its own website.

At this point in the 21st century, for quite a number of people, if something is not online, it does not exist. I do not agree with this attitude, but as in all other areas of life, survival comes through adaptation to current circumstances.[16] If a lodge wants to grow, it will need to have an online presence.

It is important to keep in mind that the man searching online for information about Freemasonry may never reach the Grand Lodge website. If he uses a search term like "freemasons avalon <state>," the first result he gets could easily be the web page for Solomon's Lodge #987![17] Consequently, it is important for the Solomon's Lodge website to be complete in and of itself. This may be your one and only opportunity to tell the truth about Freemasonry to someone, before he gets lost in the quagmire of anti-Masonic web pages and videos.

Lodge websites serve three constituencies: the members of the lodge; Masons from other lodges who are thinking of visiting the lodge; and, non-Masons trying to find out about Freemasonry. There may be pages on the website that are only for the members of the lodge (such as the calendar, resources for Masonic education, and a list of current officers and their contact information). However, from the point of view of the non-Mason, the best lodge websites will have at least these pages:

- **Home page**: This features a photograph of either the exterior of the lodge building (to help

---

[16]   In other words: "Adapt or die."

[17]   Except in Pennsylvania, where the first result will be the Facebook page of Avalon Lodge #657 F&AM. But you catch my drift, I'm sure.

people find it), the interior of the lodge room, or both (my favorite choice).[18] This page also features a physical address for the lodge, a postal address (if different), and an email address for the Secretary. It should also feature directions (by auto and by public transportation). This page features a welcome message, for current brethren, visiting brethren, and interested non-Masons. If there is a regularly scheduled activity that is open to all—such as a monthly Lodge dinner open to everyone—this should be described prominently on the website. Finally, the Home Page should explain what the other pages of the website are about.

- **What Freemasonry Is**: See my directions for the Grand Lodge website, above.

- **What Freemasonry Is Not**: See my directions for the Grand Lodge website, above.

- **Frequently Asked Questions**: See my directions for the Grand Lodge website, above.

- **Resources for Further Study**: See my directions for the Grand Lodge website, above.

- **(optional) History of Our Lodge**: It is meaningful, for members of the lodge and local non-Masons, to get a sense of how Freemasonry developed in one's home region. If you have a

---

[18] In my opinion, the website gets extra points if it has a photo of all Lodge officers in full regalia—just like, in fact, the photo on the Facebook page of Avalon Lodge #657 F&AM (GLPA). #FullOnFreemasonry

lodge history available, include a synopsis of it here. If not — write your lodge history![19]

Online Video

34. Every Grand Lodge should develop its own video channel on YouTube.

I recently had a conversation with my adult son, who stated that, when it comes to finding out or looking up information, "*always* assume that it's faster to do it online." That is certainly the standard operating assumption of the rising generations, and apparently video is preferred to text by many of the people who are of an age to petition as young adults. (My son regularly teaches himself, through online videos, how to do everything from making home improvements to cooking specialty dishes. His wife appreciates this.)

Given that this is our present reality, it behooves Grand Lodges to present the truth about Freemasonry on the media of choice for the rising generations. YouTube is not the only video platform, but it is by far the largest and — being owned by the same company that also owns the most highly used search engine, Google — YouTube videos are likely to come up first when someone Google-searches phrases like, "What is Freemasonry?" online.

What types of videos should Grand Lodge post on YouTube? Take as a guide the Five Messages of the Masonic Open House, above. Build one or more videos around each of these Five Messages, and you will have done very well indeed. Because every Grand Lodge is different, with its own

---

[19]   To know why, see Koltko-Rivera (2016).

unique history and geographical setting, it will approach these messages in different ways.

As a minimum, the Grand Lodge should have the following videos on its YouTube channel (taking my cue from the Five Messages of the Masonic Open House):

- **What is Freemasonry?** Discuss what the true character of Freemasonry is, as an initiatic fraternal society of men who are interested in becoming better men by improving their characters through symbolic and philosophical initiations and discussions. (Throw in some brief interviews with Masons of various ages, and you have already addressed the "Masonry still exists" issue.)

- **The Rumors About Freemasonry Are False.** Masonry is not a religion, a scheme for world domination, or any of that. (Enterprising Grand Lodges may have several videos along these lines.)

- **How to Become a Freemason.** Describe the process that a man follows—not the viewer, but a man in general. We are merely informing, not recruiting.

- **Masonic-affiliated organizations for women and youth.** Describe the organizations that are active in your Jurisdiction, the membership requirements of each, and how an interested person might join. (Here, too, enterprising Grand Lodges may have several videos along these lines.)

A minimum of four videos, each about 10-20 minutes in length. That requires less effort than you might think. I would guess that there are several Masons in any given Jurisdiction who each have their own YouTube channel; they can help the Grand Lodge set up their own. (Heck, there are probably De-Molays, Rainbow Girls, and Triangles who have done the same, not to forget members of the Order of the Eastern Star and the Order of the Amaranth, among other organizations.)

One might ask, why not just rely on what some other Grand Lodge has already done? Put yourself in the position of a young man residing in Mobile, Alabama, trying to find out about Freemasonry. He goes to the YouTube page, and types in a query in the search box. He then sees a long list of videos, each listed with its title and the person or group who posted it. Which of the following hypothetical videos is he most likely to click on, do you think?

- "What is Freemasonry?" Masonic Grand Lodge of New York

- "What is Freemasonry?" Secret Watchers Newsletter

- "What is Freemasonry?" Masonic Grand Lodge of California

- "What is Freemasonry?" Death to Heretics Ministries

- "What is Freemasonry?" Masonic Grand Lodge of Alabama

- "What is Freemasonry?" Occult Devil Wor-shippers Alert

- "What is Freemasonry?" Masonic Grand Lodge of Florida

Now put yourself in the position of young men residing in Saratoga, NY, San Diego, CA, and Sarasota, FL, and ask the same question.

My point is two-fold. First, men likely will seek information about Masonry that originates from a place near them before they seek such information from another Grand Lodge. Second, we Masons are up against some pretty bizarre competition when it comes to online information about Freemasonry. Better that a curious person come to us to learn about the Fraternity rather than go to that delusional competition.

35. **Grand Lodge should then ask its membership to "Subscribe" to the Grand Lodge's YouTube channel.**

This is a big deal. YouTube is more likely to recommend videos from popular channels.

36. **A Grand Lodge should ask their membership to view each of the Grand Lodge's videos all the way through, and "Like" each one (if, in fact, the brethren do).**

This is also a big deal. YouTube is more like to recommend videos that show a lot of viewer engagement (like watching it all the way through), and videos that have many viewers that have "Liked" it.

37. **On each Particular Lodge website, there should be links to the individual Grand Lodge YouTube videos.**

The "What Freemasonry Is" page of the lodge website should address each of the Five Messages of the Masonic Open House that I mentioned earlier, and it should link to the appropriate Grand Lodge YouTube videos (not just to the YouTube channel as a whole).

There are a variety of clever things that Grand Lodges can do to increase the viewership of their YouTube videos. We are talking here about search engine optimization (SEO). Certainly there are some SEO specialists within any given Jurisdiction that the Grand Lodge can rely on. At the very least, one can search phrases like "YouTube SEO" or "rank high in YouTube searches" on Google, and follow the advice given in the articles and videos that come up.

38. Particular Lodges may have their own YouTube channel, with videos that they then link to their Lodge web page.

It should go without saying that a Particular Lodge should follow the regulations and edicts that their Grand Lodge has made regarding online presence. However, if this fits with Grand Lodge regulations, it would be good for each Particular Lodge to have its own YouTube channel, featuring content that will *not* be on the typical Grand Lodge channel— such as "What Freemasonry Means to Me" video interviews with the Particular Lodge's members.

Volunteers only, please—not everyone likes to advertise the fact that he is a Freemason. But for those who are willing to put this out there—in a video that can be watched everywhere from Point Barrow, Alaska to McMurdo Station, Antarctica, from Texas to Timbuktu, from Manhattan to Melbourne—making a video like this can be a rewarding experience both for the interviewee and for the viewer. Such a video puts a personal face on Freemasonry. This is what would make Masonry real to people who otherwise know little or nothing about the Fraternity.

Addressing Some Objections

"But this is recruitment!"

For generations, American Freemasons were in the practice of sharing nothing at all about their Fraternity with non-Masons, even close family members. So widespread was this practice that anything that involved letting people know about the Fraternity smacked of recruitment.

But this is nonsense, and counterproductive of our mission. Nothing I have recommended is recruitment. Certainly we should **_not_** have a table at the Masonic Open House with posters like *Is Freemasonry for you?* or *Discover the mysteries of Freemasonry! (You know you want to!)* But no one can or will join a Fraternity that he does not know exists, or whose character he does not understand.

American Freemasons in particular need to get over their long-standing prejudice about making public statements about who and what we are. To do otherwise only plays into the hands of those who spread lies about Masonry, and furthers the trend leading to Masonic extinction.

"We don't have the personnel or resources to carry off an Open House!"

As I point out in Appendix E, a lodge can conduct a Particular Lodge Open House with about ten brothers; if a given lodge is short of personnel, it might request help from another nearby lodge. In terms of resources, the biggest necessary expenses are for the photocopying of handbills and display boards for inside the lodge, which can be obtained quite inexpensively.[20] (If financial resources are tight, skip the newspaper ads and the posters for shop windows.)

What we need to hold an Open House, more than anything else, is a willingness to exert the effort involved. We can do this.

"We do not have the Web expertise to put together the kind of website and online videos that you have described."

Certainly, a decade or two ago, custom websites and online videos would have required specialized expertise and some expensive equipment and software. However, now we live in an age of consumer technology marvels. People make and edit movies on their smartphones. The companies that will sell you an internet domain name will offer you online programs to develop your own website at low or no cost.

Some high schools require their students to produce videos for school assignments. As I mention above, one might find a wealth of video and web development talent among one's Lodge brethren, as well as DeMolay, Rainbow, and Triangle connections.

It's just not that hard anymore. We can do this.

If after all efforts are expended, a given Lodge just cannot come up with the personnel to accomplish these tasks, do not despair. Remember what Brother Theodore Roosevelt is reputed to have quoted to those complaining about the working conditions at the Panama Canal: "Do the best you can, where

---

[20] As of this writing, I see that 36-inch by 48-inch Project Display Boards are available on Amazon for under $10 apiece.

you are, with what you have." No one, certainly not I, could honestly ask for more.

What "The Four Men of Masonry" Can Do to Further the <u>Third</u> Task of the Masonic Resurgence

What the Individual Mason Can Do

There is a great deal that the individual Freemason can do to tell the world about Freemasonry.

Be as open about your Freemasonry as you are comfortable being.

The first thing you can do is to be as open about your Freemasonry as you are comfortable being. I do realize that this is a sensitive issue, which must be addressed with care.

Many brethren work in environments where it is not advantageous to be known as a Freemason. Brethren in such situations simply may not be open about their Freemasonry without jeopardizing their careers. Cabletow issues: enough said.

For other brethren, simply wearing a Masonic ring may be all they need to do, along with simply mentioning in conversation that, for example, you spent time at a Lodge BBQ over the weekend. And that alone would be fine.

Volunteer for that Open House in your Lodge.

I have recommended that each Particular Lodge hold an Open House, annually (see Recommendation #1 in this chapter). The thing with Open Houses is that, to be done really well, they do require personnel: to great visitors, to man the information tables, and so forth. (Frankly, it is very helpful to have enough personnel to man those tables and so forth in two-hour shifts.) So, make it a point to volunteer early to be part of the personnel for your Lodge's Open House.

In addition, as I have indicated earlier (Rec. #1), it is senseless to hold an Open House without publicity. Be the man who joins up for that effort early.

Volunteer to act as, or to assist, the Lodge Webmaster.

I have recommended that every Particular Lodge have its own website, and I have made Recommendations for the content of that website. (See Recommendation #25, the first Recommendation in this chapter.)

This is a big job. It is not only useful for each Lodge to have a dedicated Webmaster—an actual officer with that responsibility—but it is useful for there to be other Assistant Webmasters (to handle the contents of different pages, for example). If you have the web skills to do this, consider volunteering for service as Lodge Webmaster. Even brethren who don't have great webmaster skills may have skills at writing up content for the various pages of the website (see Rec. #33); this is prime territory for Lodge Assistant Webmasters.

Volunteer to act as, or to assist, the Lodge Videomaster.

I have recommended that, within the boundaries of Grand Lodge regulations, every Particular Lodge have its own YouTube channel, featuring videos that they then link to their Lodge web page (Recommendation #38.)

Like Lodge Webmaster, it is also a big job to be the Lodge Videomaster—that is, the brother who maintains the Lodge

YouTube channel. There is channel management, of course—fitting out the channel with a nice photo, posting and describing videos with some attention to SEO—but there is also the job of recording videos and editing them.

It is that it is not only useful for each Lodge to have a dedicated Videomaster—an actual officer with that responsibility—but it is useful for there to be other Assistants as well (to handle the production or editing of different videos, for example). If you have the video skills to do this, consider volunteering for service as Lodge Videomaster or Assistant.

This is very important. **Activities to 'Build the Lighthouse' are the most important things you can do to increase the number of petitions from worthy individuals to your Lodge.** The importance of this for the future of Freemasonry cannot be overestimated.

What the Worshipful Master Can Do

Some of the most important recommendations I have made in this chapter are completely within the capacity of the Worshipful Master to carry out—all within the boundaries of whatever regulations and policies have been set by the Grand Lodge, of course. For example, the Worshipful Master can take the initiative to discuss with his brethren the matter of holding an Open House during his term of office (Recommendation #25). In addition, if the Lodge has held tyled installations in the past, the Worshipful Master may introduce the idea of holding an open installation (Recommendation #30).

Certainly the Worshipful Master can take the initiative to raise the matter of developing a detailed website before the lodge (Recommendation #33). There are good models out there, with many educational materials for brethren.

As I mentioned above, this is very important. **Activities to 'Build the Lighthouse' are the most important things you can do to increase the number of petitions from worthy individuals to your Lodge.** The importance of this for the future of Freemasonry cannot be overestimated.

What the District Deputy Grand Master Can Do

The District Deputy Grand Master (DDGM) is uniquely situated to advance the work of the Third Task in his District. He can strongly encourage his Particular Lodges to hold Open Houses (Recommendation #25), and he can review each Lodge's plans for the same to help ensure that these will be quality experiences for all involved.

Based on the circumstances of his District, and in consultation with the Lodge Worshipful Masters therein, the DDGM can determine whether it makes sense for the lodges in his district to hold their Open Houses on the same day, or on different days distributed throughout the year (Recs. #27 and #28). Fixing the date(s) of these Open Houses is also something for which the DDGM is well situated to accomplish.

Of course, the DDGM can be crucial to the development and structure of quality websites and YouTube channels among his District's Lodges (Recommendations #33 and #38). The DDGM can promulgate Grand Lodge policies and standards, and look in on how lodges are following them.

Yes, this is very important. **Activities to 'Build the Lighthouse' are the most important things you can do to increase the number of petitions from worthy individuals to the Lodges in your District.** The importance of this for the future of Freemasonry cannot be overestimated.

What the Most Worshipful Grand Master Can Do

The Grand Master can make it a matter of policy that each Particular Lodge, individually or in cooperation with another Lodge, holds an Open House for the public, annually (Recommendation #25). The Grand Master can facilitate this by offering suggested formats for such an Open House. (Appendix E may be of assistance in this regard.)

One of the most important things a Grand Master can do is to establish an annual Masonic Day at Grand Lodge headquarters (Recommendation #29). The presence of the Grand Master can be a big draw for media attention.

In many states, there are several population centers that are at a great distance from one another (that is, at least a couple of hours of driving time). It may be wise for the Grand Master to declare an annual Masonic Day, and to preside at the ensuing activities, once at each of these population centers, of course on different dates throughout the year. This will virtually guarantee coverage in several distinct media areas.[21]

It is the prerogative of the MWGM to direct Particular Lodges to hold public installations of officers (Rec. #30).

In the area of online presence, the Grand Master can set policies that greatly facilitate the process of creating impressive and useful online presences for both the Grand Lodge and its Particular Lodges. For example, the Grand Master can

---

[21] This is clear in the two states in which I hold Masonic membership. In New York State, for example, there are very different local newspapers, radio, and television stations covering New York City, Albany, and Buffalo. In Florida, the same can be said for Jacksonville, Tallahassee, Orlando, and Miami. One can easily imagine the same being true in most states.

direct that the Grand Lodge website have a special section specifically for non-Masons, along the lines that I have suggested (Recommendations #31 and #32).

The Grand Master can decree that every Particular Lodge have its own website (Recommendation #33). In addition, he can commission guidelines for what that website should and should not include (see, for example, Recs. #37 and #38).

Under direction of the MWGM, Grand Lodge is uniquely situated to negotiate volume discounts with commercial firms to provide domain names, web hosting, and website development software to what might be hundreds of Particular Lodges in the Jurisdiction. (There are many such firms, which provide these services either singly or in combination. This provides for a healthy competition which will work to the benefit of the Grand Lodge and its Particular Lodges.)

I have recommended that every Grand Lodge and Particular Lodge should have its own YouTube online video channels, and I have recommended some policies concerning these channels (Recommendations #34-#18). I am sure it is clear that the support and direction of the Grand Master is crucial to bringing this about in a responsible manner.

Yet again, I say that this is very important. **Activities to 'Build the Lighthouse' are the most important things the MWGM can do to increase the number of petitions from worthy individuals to Lodges in his Jurisdiction.** The importance of this for the future of Freemasonry cannot be over-estimated.

11

The Fourth Task: <u>Repair the Western Gate</u>

Deal Properly with Interested Persons and Petitioners

Among the five major reasons for the Masonic decline that I identified in Chapter 6 above ("American Freemasonry Today"), the fourth was that we may be bringing in some inappropriate candidates. In this chapter, we directly address this problem.

The Fourth Task of the Masonic resurgence is to Repair the Western Gate. By this, I mean that the Lodge needs to deal properly with people who are interested in Freemasonry, and with actual Petitioners. This interaction has these objectives:

A. We wish all persons interested in the Fraternity to have an accurate understanding of Freemasonry's character: who we are, and what we stand for.

B. We wish all persons petitioning the Fraternity to understand what the focuses of Freemasonry really are, to understand and assent to what will be expected of them as a Freemason.

C. We absolutely wish all persons petitioning the Fraternity to be of good moral character.

There are several 'moving parts' involved in fulfilling these objectives, and we will consider them one at a time.

A. Dealing with Members of the Public Who Are Interested in Freemasonry

Members of the public who are curious about or interested in Freemasonry may express that curiosity or interest in different ways. Some may drop in at a stall or table set up by Brethren at some public event (like an public recreational or cultural festival). Others may present themselves at a Lodge event open to the public, such as a recreational or social event, or an open dinner.

39. Particular Lodges should establish a standardized response for their brethren to give to inquiries from the general public, received at Lodge events.

It is important in such circumstances to have a fairly standardized response. I recommend the following approach be used when someone in the general public asks about 'who the Masons are,' or 'is it true what I hear about the Freemasons,' or some such:

a) Straightforwardly but briefly state something to the effect that "Freemasonry is a fraternity that focuses on self-improvement. In connection with that, we sometimes give our effort to service and charitable projects as well. As a fraternity, of course we meet and fellowship with each other."

Note: this is all of three sentences. That's it. The language is plain, accurate, and appropriate for people who do not know anything about the Fraternity. We don't have to go 'deep into the weeds' here.

Should someone happen to ask about what we mean by 'self-improvement,' one can follow this up with another brief response, such as, "We use symbols and lectures to get across messages about how people could better behave and treat each other, and how they can better relate to the Divine." If the questioner then asks for further details, it is appropriate to say that to go into further detail would involve going into the ritual itself, which we treat as confidential.

b) "What have you heard about Freemasonry?"

c) The brother can then clear up any of the myriad bizarre misconceptions that they might mention they have heard. Again: simply, straightforwardly, without going into deep discourse.

There is no recruitment here. What we have here is a clear and straightforward, yet very brief statement of what Freemasonry is. Someone who is not interested in self-improvement should be able to take this message away from the outset: "This is not for me." This could easily be one less NPD down the road.

B. Dealing with People Who Express an Interest in Petitioning the Lodge

Though it should go without saying, yet it still needs to be said: **No one should be invited** to submit a petition to receive the mysteries of Freemasonry.[22]

That said, of course men do express a desire to petition to become Freemasons, by the thousands, every year. When this happens, we have three great concerns to be answered, two of them *before any petition should be offered:*

A. Is this person really interested in the Fraternity as it is in reality, rather than some fantasy?

B. Will this person perform his duties as a Freemason?

C. Is this person truly of good moral character? (This question is traditionally answered after a petition is actually submitted.)

We shall address Questions A and B here, and Question C in the following section.

40. A Particular Lodge should assign brothers to have an interview with someone interested in submitting a petition—*before* any petition is offered.

---

[22] I do realize that some Grand Lodges have exceptions to this policy. I am merely expressing my opinion in relation to this issue. It would seem appropriate, with someone who has many questions about, and a favorable and accurate impression of, the Fraternity might be told the following two sentences: "Freemasonry does not recruit. Someone who is interested in becoming a Freemason must ask all on his own." I strongly suggest that we **leave it at that**.

In this pre-petition interview, the brothers should be careful to inquire into the following:

- What does the interested party think that Freemasonry is?

- What does he think Freemasonry is *about?*

- What does he think Masons do?

At this point, the brethren conducting the interview should inform the interested party about the true nature of Freemasonry, as a fraternity that is primarily concerned with the moral and spiritual improvement of its members. We conduct highly symbolic initiation rituals in which we convey values that we should show in our behavior towards others, and we convey a few powerful lessons about a man's relationship to the Divine. In our meetings, we present educational sessions in which we teach ourselves how to better live up to those values.[23] We also conduct lodge business in these meetings. As a fraternity, of course we fellowship with each other. What we are *not* is a society for networking in order to further one's business or career interests.

The brethren conducting the interview should also indicate what would be expected of the interested party as a Mason. First, that he will keep the details of our initiations confidential and secure. Second, that he will accept every Lodge member as a Brother, regardless of age, race, ethnic background, social standing, or any other social quality. Third, that

---

[23]   Frankly, any lodge where this is not true will not keep the interest of the interested party for long after initiation.

he will not discuss politics or religion in the Lodge.[24] <u>Fourth</u>, that he will actually *attend* Lodge meetings, both Stated and Special Communications, unless his health, family responsibilities, or work responsibilities demand otherwise.[25] These four expectations are not negotiable, and all are mandatory.

Finally, the brethren conducting the interview should explain that submitting a petition does not automatically result in a person being admitted to initiation. If the Lodge will be performing a criminal background check (which I strongly recommend it does), this should be made clear to the interested party—as well as the cost to him, over and above initiation fees. It should also be made clear that certain offenses will result in automatic rejection of a petition; what these offenses are should be spelled out (see below).

It may well be the case that this is not all agreeable to the interested party. In that case, it behooves the brethren conducting the interview to be very amiable in thanking the interested party for his interest, and to wish him well in his endeavors and his life's journey.

---

[24] I like to explain that this means not discussing politics or religion in "any Masonic context," including dinners, informal gatherings before or after Lodge meetings, Lodge recreational and social events, etc.

[25] I would attend Lodge on my birthday. I would *not* attend Lodge on my spouse's or child's birthday, or on my wedding anniversary or Valentine's Day (which, in the United States, has the status of a quasi-official national couple's holiday). I have heard of brothers who have skipped out on lodge for recreational or sporting events, which I think is quite juvenile. On the other hand, I have heard of a brother who was strongly pressured by a Masonic relative to cut his honeymoon short to attend lodge; this borders on fanaticism.

But that is all. There should be absolutely no attempt to minimize any of the issues mentioned above. There is no need to say, "call us if you change your mind." We do not court potential Petitioners; it is they who must court Freemasonry.

> **41. Each Particular Lodge should establish a "getting to know you" process—extending over some months—that must be completed before an interested party may submit a Petition.**

Should the interested party be agreeable to what has been discussed in the interview, this still should not mean that a petition should be presented. There should be a "getting to know you" process before someone is allowed to petition the Lodge, and this process should be clearly explained to the interested party at the pre-Petition interview.

It is wise to require the interested party to attend lodge events (obviously outside the Stated Communication), for a certain number of events over several months, before this person may file a petition. This may involve Lodge dinners, recreational events, or social events, including informal "hangouts" with lodge members.

These events allow the interested party to show his commitment to actually "showing up." It allows the Lodge brothers to reinforce the message of what Freemasonry is really about—a fierce commitment to personal moral improvement—in private conversations. It also allows Lodge members to ascertain to what extent the interested party already has a commitment to inner development and self-improvement.

At the conclusion of the period set by the Lodge for "getting to know you" activities—some Lodges will choose, say, six months—the Lodge can decide whether an opportunity to file a Petition should be extended.

42. Each Particular Lodge should hold a "Preparation for Initiation" meeting with successful Petitioners.

After submitting a Petition, and after a clear ballot has been returned in the Lodge, but before initiation, a Petitioner should continue to attend lodge events aside from the Stated Communication. This would be a good time to prepare the Petitioner for initiation through an explanation of the mental and even spiritual preparation that he should undergo in order to be better prepared for the initiation experience.

But there remains one question to be answered before actual initiation.

C. Ensuring Good Moral Character in Our Petitioners

In an earlier time, it was considered sufficient to ask for a Petitioner to secure character references. In smaller rural communities, the chances were good that some member of the Lodge actually knew the people rendering the character reference. However, recent times have demonstrated the need to take things a bit farther.

The fact of the matter is that I have known candidates to be accepted into Lodges, when they had hidden criminal records that emerged only later. Sometimes this has resulted in very unfortunate incidents.

All of this leads me to make this strong Recommendation:

43. Submit every Petitioner to a criminal background check.

Tell him in advance that this will be happening—and make it clear back at the pre-Petition interview that he is to pay for it.

Now, times change, and things that might have been considered serious offenses are not so considered today. For example, I would <u>not</u> exclude a Petitioner who had been convicted of personal possession or use of small amounts of marijuana. I <u>definitely would</u> exclude a Petitioner who had committed and been convicted of a violent felony, a hate crime, any form of abuse, anything that would land a person on a registry of sex offenders, drug or human trafficking, or major white-collar crime.

In between is a vast gray area, and every Lodge must decide for itself how to treat Petitioners who do not present with a clean record. Preferably, a Lodge sets its standards in advance. It makes perfectly good sense to judge each Petitioner in the context of his whole life (aside from certain automatic exclusions, such as those that I describe above).

Ah, But What About ...

Now for a tough area, which we really must consider head-on: What about an interested party who is a White nationalist or a neo-Nazi? On the one hand, we are not to take personal politics into consideration when deciding whether to advance a Petitioner to Candidate status. On the other hand ..., good gosh, we're talking Nazis here.

I offer the following as my personal opinion only. It is, however, a reasoned position, and one which builds itself on core Masonic values.

44. I would not consider any man who holds to a philosophy of racial exclusion or racial superiority to be a fit candidate for Freemasonry.

One of the core values of Freemasonry is *egalitarianism*. Within Masonry, this takes the position that all men, of whatever religion, race, ethnic background, or vocation, are equally brothers and should be treated equally. Unlike other political parties, White nationalist parties and neo-Nazi movements reject this premise from the start; indeed, the rejection of the egalitarian premise is the very core of their philosophy.

It does not matter whether Pythagoras-Platonic Lodge #3997 happens to be composed completely of White Christians of Northern and Western European descent. As a Masonic lodge, it is bound to uphold Masonic values; in principle, it must accept into its meetings otherwise well-recommended Jewish, Muslim, or Buddhist Masons from Trinidad and Tobago, Tunisia, Turkmenistan, Tokyo, Tel-Aviv, and the vicinity of Lake Titicaca. White Nationalists and neo-Nazis, by the very fact of their affiliations, cannot accept such men as Brothers. Therefore, in my estimate, we cannot accept White Nationalists or neo-Nazis of any stripe as Brothers, either.

Tattoos such as "88," "14/88," "Fourteen Words," and "HH" should all raise questions in this regard when seen on an interested party or Petitioner.[26]

---

[26] The letter "H" is the 8th letter of the alphabet; "88" is sometimes used as a code to reference "HH," the initials of the phrase "Heil Hitler." The so-called Fourteen Words, in one version, run as follows: "We must secure the existence of our people and a future for white children" —excluding a future for children of any other race, and so forth.

Addressing an Objection

"Good gosh, man! With all that interviewing and waiting, you will scare off potential candidates before they can even petition!"

Consider again *why* I have made these recommendations: the Masonic membership crisis. We seem to have been admitting some candidates who are really not interested in what Masonry is about. These men do not contribute to the atmosphere of a vibrant lodge, and then they leave. Better that they do not come into the Fraternity to start with.

What we want are Lodges composed all of men who really want to be there, to do the things that Masons are supposed to do. Such Lodges are more fulfilling, and more encouraging to be in, for everyone involved.

What "The Four Men of Masonry" Can Do to Further the <u>Fourth</u> Task of the Masonic Resurgence

What the Individual Mason Can Do

For the recommendations that I have made to work, many individual Masons need to volunteer to conduct the "interested party" pre-Petition interviews, as well as the "Preparation for Initiation" training. Be the Mason who volunteers to his Worshipful Master to do this.

What the Worshipful Master Can Do

It is in the Worshipful Master's power to take the initiative to institute such practices as I have recommended here. Because my recommendations probably represent a serious departure from business as usual, it would be best to do this with the full support of the Wardens, Trustees, and the Lodge as a whole.

What the District Deputy Grand Master Can Do

The RW DDGM can encourage Lodges in his District to carry out the program I have recommended here, and to help them to carry it out. Of course, he cannot *insist* that these Lodges institute such a program.

What the Most Worshipful Grand Master Can Do

On the other hand, the MW Grand Master *can* insist that the Lodges of the Jurisdiction carry out such a program as I have recommended here. Yes, there will probably be fewer initiations the first year or so that this program is put in place. I believe that this drop will not only be temporary, but will be heavily outweighed by having Lodges filled with more committed Masons who do not drop out of the Fraternity a little ways down the road.

12

The Fifth Task: <u>Build the Guard Towers</u>

Defend Freemasonry

Among the five major reasons for the Masonic decline that I identified in Chapter 6 above ("American Freemasonry Today"), the fifth was that, in many cases, anti-Masonic propaganda discourages the honest in heart from investigating Freemasonry. This lowers the number of petitions we receive, I think rather seriously. I think this, in part, because it certainly got in the way of *my* petition, as I will explain below. The fact of the matter is that a substantial portion of the American public believe that Masonry is a Satanic, devil-worshipping conspiracy that is bent on enslaving humanity. This certainly inhibits our growth, because it directly discourages people from petitioning; in addition, family members and friends who believe such vile lies may discourage a person from submitting a petition, or may even encourage an initiated brother to drop out of the Fraternity.

In this chapter, we directly address this problem. The Fifth Task of the Masonic resurgence is to Build the Guard Towers. By this, I mean that we should defend Freemasonry, boldly, and in public.

The Masonic Custom of Ignoring "Criticism"[27]

Freemasons have long made it a practice not to respond to aspersions cast upon the Fraternity. The late Masonic historian, Henry Wilson Coil, noted that "... the [premier] Grand Lodge ... from the outset, established a custom, now universally recognized, of never responding to critics and of refusing to be drawn into fights. (Coil, 1996, p. 54, s.v. "Anti-Masonry").

Over time, this "custom" became solidified into an attitude all but prohibiting responses to anti-Masonry. For example, in the Charge given to me as a new Entered Apprentice, I heard the following:

> Although your frequent appearance at our Communications is earnestly solicited, yet it is not meant that Masonry should interfere with your necessary vocations; for these are on no account to be neglected; *neither are you to suffer your zeal for the institution to lead you into argument with those who, through ignorance, may ridicule it.* (*Florida Masonic Monitor*, 1995, p. 63)[28]

This message was further emphasized to me in materials I received soon after I was initiated, in what I shall refer to hereafter as the *Booklet #1* statement:

---

[27] Some of the following sections are based on Koltko-Rivera (2007).

[28] Substantially the same wording is given in *Monitors* previously used in New York and Texas (Grand Lodge of Free and Accepted Masons of the State of New York, 1958, pp. 23-24; Lightfoot, 1934. pp. 38-39).

What is a Mason to do in response to attacks from outside? ...

> Our attitude toward such attacks is to ignore them. We do not fight back. We take the position that if some man (or group of men) disagrees with the teachings of Freemasonry, that is his own private affair and does not concern us. We do nothing to invite, or to warrant such attacks, therefore they are no affair of ours. Our faith in the truth and right of Freemasonry is so well-founded that we are certain it needs to do nothing except go on being itself in order to silence sooner or later any charges that may be made against it by any kind of enemies. (Grand Lodge of Florida, 1994, pp. 10-11)

As admirable a statement as this is, in its respect for the Fraternity, it has some serious flaws. The *Booklet #1* statement assumes that if someone is attacking Masonry, it is simply because that someone "disagrees with the teachings of Freemasonry." That certainly did happen—centuries ago.

It may be difficult to believe this in the 21st century, but several of the core values and practices of Freemasonry were the subject of hot debate in Europe when the first Grand Lodge was established. "One person, one vote"? Why. this would lead to 'republicanism,' where the people would hold sovereignty, not the Crown! Religious tolerance? An offense against the One True Faith! The idea of all men being "on the level"? That violates the natural privileges of the aristocracy! A respect for so-called 'science' and 'logic'? An attack on the privileges of the traditional teachings of the Church! *Quelle horreur*, indeed!

In that context, sure, it made perfectly good sense for the premier Grand Lodge to assert the policy of not responding to critics of Freemasonry. Direct engagement with such critics would simply have led to the sorts of religious and political disputes that we were trying to keep *out* of the Lodges.

However, modern anti-Masonry has little to do with 18th-century disagreements, most of which have long since been settled in favor of the Masonic positions, at least in the countries of Europe, the Americas, and Australia (the majority of which are republics with religious freedom). In today's anti-Masonry, the stakes are much higher—and far, far weirder.

The Grotesque World of Today's Anti-Masonry

In 2016, I took two snapshots of Freemasonry as it existed online. I looked at two things: (1) the first 100 Web pages found in a Google search of the term "Freemasonry," and (2) the first 100 videos found by searching the same term on YouTube. The results were quite troubling:

- One-fifth (20%) of the top-ranked web page results were clearly anti-Masonic in nature.

- Fully half (51%) of the top-ranked YouTube video results were clearly anti-Masonic in nature.

The anti-Masonic websites basically depicted Freemasonry as a Satanic conspiracy, bent on instituting totalitarian rule in the New World Order. Here are the titles of some representative examples of the anti-Masonic web pages:

- "The Aim of Freemasonry is the Triumph of Communism."

- "Freemasons – The silent destroyers. Deist religious cult."

- "Freemasons Exposed!" (Description: "The gods of the Freemasonry lodge [*sic*] are Egyptian gods.")

- "Freemasonry: Midwife to an Occult Empire." (Description: "Evidence that the higher Masonic degrees conceal the true nature of Freemasonry as a Satanic religion.")

If anything, these themes were picked up even more sharply in the anti-Masonic YouTube videos, of which these titles are representative:

- "Join freemasonry & lose your soul (proof)."

- "Secrets of Freemasonry found in masonic books." (Description: "Lucifer is the god of Freemasonry and other facts written by high ranking masons in their own books that are found in libraries ....")

- "The Secret Agenda of High Level Freemasonry."

- "Illuminati The Freemasonry [*sic*] and Zionism – The Master Plan to Rule the World."

- "Why Won't Celebrities Tell Their Illuminati Freemasonry Secrets?"

- "Freemasonry: A Jewish Luciferian Cult (a rare daring investigation)."

- "Baphomet is the 'God' of Freemasonry."

- "Freemasonry, Masonic Lodge and the Shriners Are Not Compatible with Biblical Christianity."

- "Lucifer Worshippers Exposed!!! Plotting SOON World takeover!!! Illuminati – Jesuits – Freemasonry."

The nine videos above had a combined total of 804,296 views on the date of my review. (Individual videos ranged from 5,508 to 191,882 views.) Some anti-Masonic videos in the YouTube top-ranked 100 have had ***over one million views—apiece.*** (The #1-ranked video on "Freemasonry" contended that the Fraternity is an ongoing indoctrination into Satanism. This video alone had over two million views. Its title: "Watch THIS Before Joining Freemasonry!")

Of course, this insanity appears in print, as well. A few years ago, I picked up a book at one of my local chain bookstores, by a best-selling author who propagated accusations of wide-spread Masonic child abuse—supposed perpetrated during Lodge ritual!—as well as the news that each Lodge building was connected by a tunnel system to the secret subterranean bases of hostile space aliens. One might just dismiss this as pure insanity in print; however, this particular insanity, by an internationally best-selling author, is selling briskly to a large crowd of people who apparently believe what this man has to tell. Are we really to say nothing in response to this?

The upshot of all this is that when a potential candidate goes online or to a bookstore to find out information about the Fraternity, a substantial proportion of what he encounters will be, not just misinformed inaccuracies, but melodramatic delusions of the most lurid sort. Should he look for online videos on the topic—the preferred method of the rising generation, it seems—then the search for truth may be aborted at the very beginning, because of the flood of highly developed but delusional and bizarre falsehoods about Freemasonry that are easily available on the Internet.

We must not tolerate this any longer. We must directly counter the grotesque and often sickening lies told about Freemasonry—lies that I believe keep many good men from the Fraternity.

I have good reason to believe this—because *I* was one of those men who were kept from the Fraternity by anti-Masonic propaganda. My petition to a Masonic lodge was put off by perhaps as much as twenty years, as a result of reading the false accusations against Freemasonry advanced by the notorious Stephen Knight in his popular book *The Brotherhood*. Sometimes I think about what I could have accomplished as a Mason in those twenty years. We all should think about the many men who might otherwise have been truly great Masons, had they not been led astray by anti-Masonry—an anti-Masonry that we have often abstained from responding to, based on outmoded policies rooted in 17th-century realities, rather than in the world of the 21st century.

A Stance for 21st Century Freemasonry

Many of the accusations made against Masonry in our era are particularly salacious and twisted. In the face of such accusations, it is our duty and responsibility to stand up for Masonry, not only by maintaining our proper conduct, but by actively responding to the accusations made against us, many of which accusations are hideous in the extreme.

To abstain from responding to distortions and lies is not a stance of nobility and virtue; rather, this practice leaves us open to having others apply to us the interpretation propounded in a tenet of the English common law, namely, that "silence is assent." That is, by our silence, we let others infer

that the accusations against us are true. And, in the 21ˢᵗ century, those accusations are truly heinous.

To put it bluntly, to take the position that 'one needs do
nothing in the face of accusations because truth will out' is, in
our age, at best naïve, and at worst outright dangerous. Defending our reputation is, at the least, due diligence.

There is an alternative perspective that we might take on
the Masonic ethics of responding to anti-Masonry: namely,
that we *ought* to respond to it, as shown by our own core
teachings. This is evidenced by looking at, not the Charge giv-
en to the EA, but the Charge given to the new Master Mason:

> To preserve unsullied the reputation of the Fra-
> ternity ought to be your constant care ....
> [E]ndeavor to remove every aspersion against
> this venerable institution. (*Florida Masonic Moni-
> tor*, 1995, pp. 126-127)

> You are now bound by duty, honor, and grat-
> itude ... to support the dignity of your character
> on every occasion .... To preserve the reputation
> of the Fraternity unsullied must be your constant
> care. ... Demand respectful treatment from your
> neighbor .... Make others to know always that a
> gentleman stands before them. (Grand Lodge of
> Free and Accepted Masons of the State of New
> York, 1958, pp. 51-54)[29]

It is the duty of the Master Mason to stand up for the reputation of the Fraternity. Never has Masonry more needed its
Masters to stand up for it than right now. Mitch Horowitz, the

---

[29] About the first half of this is also found in Lightfoot (1934), p. 92.

editor of one of my previous books (*Freemasonry: An Introduction*) put it well: **#DefendMasonry**.

How We Can Defend Freemasonry

So, how might Masons go about the task of defending the Fraternity? There is so much that we can do.

I have mentioned the following ideas in Chapter 10 ("… Tell the World About Freemasonry"):

- A portion of every lodge open house may be devoted to correcting misinformation about Freemasonry.

- Lodges and Grand Lodges may devote pages of their websites to correcting misinformation and rumors about Freemasonry.

This alone would help to correcting misinformation—but it is not enough by a long shot. We need to take the fight to the enemy, so to speak—by responding directly to anti-Masonry where it is most frequently encountered: on YouTube.

45. Individual Masons should comment in defense of Masonry on anti-Masonic videos on the YouTube platform, in a brief but effective manner.

Informed Masons need to respond directly in their comments to anti-Masonic videos on YouTube. An excellent response would be to do the following:

A. State that the video is wrong.

B. State, *very briefly*, just *how* the video is wrong. There are so many different kinds of wrong that a video can be. It might be based on a forgery. It might be based on a misrepresentation of Masonic ritual, vocabulary, or practice. It may simply be based on *nothing*, but just be some fantasy that someone has made up out of thin air, or repeated. If you can put it into a single, brief sentence, state the 'category of wrong' that this video represents.

C. <u>Link to a website or video that lays out the truth about this particular topic.</u>

That last step is crucial. The bald assertion that something is wrong is not enough. One must back this up with facts. Yet, it is most efficient to do this by referring to another place on the internet—a page of text or a video—that has this laid out.

So, where would you find such pages? I would suggest the essays and papers found at the following locations (not in any order of preference):

- The magnificent website of the Grand Lodge of British Columbia and Yukon:

  http://freemasonry.bcy.ca/texts/index.html

  These brethren have rendered an invaluable service to all of Freemasonry by collecting over one hundred essays, papers, and articles on many aspects of the Fraternity. Although the material connected under the heading "Anti-masonry" is the most obviously relevant, there are several other headings where relevant material appears such as "Biography," "History," "Of masonic interest," "Other societies," "Religion," and "Symbolism."

- Bro. Edward L. King's monumental website, "Anti-Masonry Points of View":

  http://www.masonicinfo.com/

  Here are dozens of pages about objections to Free-masonry, those who oppose Freemasonry—as well as just plain information about Freemasonry itself. Bro. King has rendered a truly great service to the Fraternity by collecting—and authoring many of— these resources; don't be shy about using it.

- The online article "Difficult Questions About Free-masonry" by Roger Firestone, on Gary L. Dryfoos terrific site, "A Page About Freemasonry":

  http://web.mit.edu/dryfoo/www/Masonry/
      Questions/difficult.html

  This excellent essay addresses clearly and in one place a number of misconceptions about Freema-sonry. (There is a great deal of great information about Freemasonry on Bro. Dryfoos' page.)

- If your home Lodge or Grand Lodge has a page devoted to responses to anti-Masonry—and I strongly recommend that they should—I suggest that you link to those pages.

- Over time, I will be adding videos on responding to anti-Masonry on the YouTube channel, "The Re-surgence of Freemasonry": https://bit.ly/2LN7whz You may wish to link to appropriate videos at this channel.

Although the first time you do this it might take a few minutes to find the right videos to link to, over time you will find that you develop a feel (and perhaps a list) for the videos that you most need to link to.

That's it. Your response only need be ***three sentences long***. Yet that small investment of effort can make a great difference in whether someone sees an anti-Masonic video as true or false.

How do you select which videos to comment on first? See Recommendation #46, below.

Addressing Some Objections

"You'll never convince the hard-core anti-Masons of anything opposed to their prejudices!"

That's fine. That is not what I'm trying to do anyway.

On any given matter of debate, except for extraordinarily polarizing issues, the distribution of public opinion tends to resemble a bell curve. About a sixth of the public tends to be extremely committed to the "pro" side of the issue, and about a sixth of the public tends to be extremely committed to the "con" side of the issue. *And you do not care about changing the opinions of people who sit at these extremes.*

The people whom you are trying to reach are the two-thirds of people in the middle, who have milder commitments to one or the other side of the issue. In particular, you are trying to reach the half of this group—which amounts to one-third of the whole population—who simply have no strong opinion either way. These are the people who check the "Don't Know" response in opinion polls.

Most importantly for our purposes, **this is the group that contains most of the people who are just trying to learn more about Masonry in the first place**. This is the group that contains the honest-in-heart seekers after truth who tend to become our best Petitioners anyway—if they can find their way through the forest of anti-Masonic videos to the clearing in the forest where they can learn the truth about the Fraternity.

So don't worry about changing the opinions of the hard-core anti-Masonic fanatics who post these videos that you will be commenting on. Don't be concerned about changing the opinions of their hard-core followers, either. *Do* be concerned about reaching those of their viewers who *are* simply trying to find out the truth, and just stumbled upon these anti-Masonic videos.

"It doesn't matter how you respond to anti-Masonic videos! The authors of those videos will just delete your comments or close their videos to comments altogether!"

Don't be so sure about that.

Yes, it is true that some video authors may delete comments that contradict their videos. If that happens, you will only have put in three sentences' worth of work into your comment, so little of your work will be wasted. (Actually, none of your work will be wasted, if you keep a file of your responses, so that you can reuse them with other videos on the same topic.)

But it is important to keep in mind that your comments on those videos may not be deleted at all. Video authors vary very widely in how diligent they are about monitoring the comments on their videos. Some may never bother to look at your comments. Some may have stopped maintaining their channels at all, having changed their interests. Not to be morbid, but some video authors simply die and leave their videos up for posterity.

The thing to take away from this is that your comments will be seen for as long as they are seen: for a day, a week, or perhaps many years. It is worth the effort to make them.

"But the authors will simply respond back, saying something like 'Oh, but that is what we would *expect* a Mason to say!'"

And if the authors do respond back that way, there is a simple, brief, and I dare say elegant, retort that you can use. When I have had such responses, I have usually found the following to be a good way to end that kind of discussion:

> All that you are doing is declaring that you really have nothing to say here at all. You have not said anything to rebut the facts that I have presented at all (including the link). You have just given the weakest possible response: a circular argument. You claimed that the Masons are untrustworthy; when a Mason speaks up with evidence showing that you are wrong, you say that this evidence can't be trusted—because the Masons are untrustworthy. Circular arguments are a sign that you really don't have anything to present to rebut what I have said. You are all out of ammunition, as it were.

Again, remember that you aren't writing this for the video's author, but rather for the sake of the audience.

"There are just too many anti-Masonic videos on YouTube to respond to! You can't hope to respond to them all!"

Let's consider the facts.

A quick Google search of videos related to "Freemasonry" (11 August 2018) showed that they estimated "about 833,000 results," about 40% of them being YouTube videos. If my estimate that about half of YouTube videos are anti-Masonic in nature is accurate, that means that there are over 166,000 anti-Masonic videos on YouTube as of this date—and more are being uploaded every day. That is, of course, a truly massive, all but inconceivable number of videos.

But let us apply some scientific principles here. In the 1940s, the Romanian-born American engineer Joseph M. Juran stumbled on the work of 19th century Italian economist Vilfredo Pareto, who formulated what we now call the "Pareto principle," "the law of the vital few"—and the 80/20 rule. Applying that rule here, it implies that 80% of the damage to Freemasonry inflicted by *all* anti-Masonic YouTube videos is caused by only 20% of them. We do our best to concentrate, not on all 166,000 videos, but only on about 33,200 of them. That is still a large number, but responding to this many videos is much more achievable than trying to respond to the entire number.

But let's not stop there. Look at it this way. Let us say that an average of only 1% of Freemasons each put in a single hour weekly responding to anti-Masonic videos. Right now, that would amount to about 9,000 hours of effort, or 4.5 man-years of effort, put into this task—*weekly*. That is about 220 man-years of effort, put into this effort, every single year. How many videos could these brethren respond to, and how much time would it take to do that?

Let us say that, once a Mason is up to speed on this task, in that hour of weekly effort, that Mason is responding to anti-Masonic videos at the rate of only 3 videos per hour. That would mean that, after the learning curve, 1% of all Masons would be responding to 27,000 videos a yea.

That's right. We would have responded to the major anti-Masonic videos in *__less than 18 months__* — a year and a half.

So, how does one choose the top 20% of YouTube videos to respond to? That is the easiest part of this whole effort.

46. Use the YouTube algorithm to help decide what anti-Masonic videos to comment on.

The YouTube people go to a huge amount of effort to deliver, in search results and suggestions, 'the right video to the right person at the right time,' as I've heard some experts put it. So, if you do a YouTube search of the term "Freemasonry," you will see a list of results that, from the top down, combine several qualities, including relevance, popularity, and recency. They are the videos on the topic that have been *__most popular recently__*. This explains why the videos are not listed simply in descending order of number of views, or simply in chronological order, most recent first.

If someone posted a video two years ago about how Freemasons are devil-worshippers — and, trust me, there are a lot of those videos out there — and 5,000 people watched that video during *this month*, that video will rank higher than more recent videos who were watched by more people five months ago. (YouTube has an algorithm that it tweaks 200 to 300 times a year to parse out all the possible factors involved in recommending what videos to list as results to your search.)

All of this suggests a plan of action:

- On your computer, open your web browser, but either in an *incognito window* (for PCs) or a *private window* (for Macs). (This is important, because in this mode, YouTube will not take into account your usual web browsing habits. Otherwise, if you watch a lot of videos that offer legitimate instruction about Freemasonry, you will get a lot of positive videos about Freemasonry in your list. Opening an incognito or private window will force your YouTube search to assume you are a "typical" viewer—which is just what you want.)

- Go to YouTube, and search the word "Freemasonry."

- Of the list presented to you, start at the top, and look for an anti-Masonic video. (Unfortunately, this will only take seconds.)

- Take the first one, and comment on it as I have recommended above.

What if another Mason has already commented on this video? First of all, if you approve of his comment, by all means "Like" it. Beyond that, see whether you can add something original in a comment of your own, especially regarding the link you could post. Perhaps the Brother who commented earlier linked to one online article or video, but you could link to another. Go right on ahead and do so. It only does good to let the video's viewers know that people can rebut this video from several angles.

What "The Four Men of Masonry" Can Do to Further the <u>Fifth</u> Task of the Masonic Resurgence

What the Individual Mason Can Do

The individual Mason can do a great deal to defend Masonry. Some things that address topics I have mentioned in earlier chapters include:

- Volunteering to the Worshipful Master to man the display at the Lodge Open House that deals with responding to some of the negative myths about Freemasonry.

- Volunteering to the Worshipful Master to find or compose appropriate materials and links to respond to some of these negative myths, on a special page of the Lodge website.

But in addition to these important tasks, there is one further place in which the individual Masons can make a great impact: cyberspace. The individual Mason can follow the three-step program that I outlined above at Recommendation #45 to respond to anti-Masonic videos: on a video-by-video basis, (A) state that the video is wrong, (B) state, very briefly, just how the video is wrong, and (C) link to a website or video that lays out the truth about this particular topic. (See Recommendation #46 to see how to select videos to respond to.)

I know what you might be thinking: what possible difference can one Mason make? As it happens, this is very much like voting: what difference can one vote make? And, in each case, this is the wrong way to look at the issue.

Both in voting and in responding to anti-Masonic videos, it's not what *just one* person can do, but what *just a small proportion of people* can do. And, as it happens, just a small proportion of people is usually all that's needed to swing quite a lot of elections one way or the other, even on the national level.

Look at it this way. I have estimated above that if only 1% of Freemasons each put in a single hour weekly responding to anti-Masonic videos, that is about 220 man-years of effort, put into this effort, every single year. I have also estimated that the 1% of Masons could respond to the 20% of anti-Masonic videos that does 80% of the damage that videos do to the Fraternity in *less than 18 months*. **That** is what a very small proportion of Freemasons can do.

Put in those terms, one can see that an exceptional Mason here, with an exceptional Mason there, can make a very great deal of difference.

So be part of the one-hour-a-week army that responds to anti-Masonic videos (all within appropriate Grand Lodge guidelines, if any). You can do a great deal of good.

What the Worshipful Master Can Do

The WM can do a great deal to further this effort. Some things that address topics I have mentioned in earlier chapters include:

- Putting on an annual Open House in the Lodge, including a display that deals with responding to some of the negative myths about Freemasonry.

- Commissioning a Lodge website, including a page with appropriate materials and links to respond to some of these negative myths.

Beyond this, the WM can encourage brethren to take part in the one-hour-a-week effort that I have outlined above, regarding responding to anti-Masonic videos. If even just one or two brethren in each Lodge took it upon themselves to do this, across many Lodges this would add up to a huge effort.

What the District Deputy Grand Master Can Do

The DDGM can also do a great deal to further this effort. Some things that address topics I have mentioned in earlier chapters include:

- Encouraging the Lodges in your District to put on an annual Open House in their Lodges, including a display that deals with responding to some of the negative myths about Freemasonry.

- Encouraging the Lodges in your District to each have a Lodge website, including a page with appropriate materials and links to respond to some of these negative myths.

Beyond this, the DDGM can encourage the brethren in his District to take part in the one-hour-a-week effort that I have outlined above, regarding responding to anti-Masonic videos. As I mentioned above to Worshipful Masters, if even just one or two brethren in each Lodge took it upon themselves to do this, across many Lodges this adds up to a great deal of effort. This is easier to see from the perspective of a DDGM, where the efforts of one or two brethren in each Lodge could add up to ten to twenty or more hours of effort weekly.

What the Most Worshipful Grand Master Can Do

The MW Grand Master can have a massive impact in furthering this effort. Some things that address topics I have mentioned in earlier chapters include:

- Hold an annual Masonic Day at Grand Lodge—essentially, an Open House writ large—including displays and perhaps a talk that deal with responding to some of the negative myths about Freemasonry.

- Have your Grand Lodge website include a section with appropriate materials and links to respond to some of these negative myths.

- Encouraging the Lodges in your Jurisdiction to put on an annual Open House in their Lodges, including a display that deals with responding to some of the negative myths about Freemasonry.

- Encouraging the Lodges in your Jurisdiction to each have a Lodge website, including a page with appropriate materials and links to respond to some of these negative myths.

Beyond this, the MWGM can encourage the brethren in his Jurisdiction to take part in the one-hour-a-week effort that I have outlined above, regarding responding to anti-Masonic videos. As I mentioned above to Worshipful Masters and DDGMs, if even just one or two brethren in each Lodge took it upon themselves to do this, across many Lodges this adds up to a great deal of effort. This is especially easy to see from the perspective of a Grand Lodge, where the efforts of one or two brethren in each Lodge could add up to hundreds, even thousands of hours of effort weekly, in this crucial effort.

The MWGM can also take the step of commissioning the development of "Recommended Responses" for brethren to use in commenting on anti-Masonic videos—brief, three-sentence responses along the lines of the three parts of a comment mentioned in Recommendation #45.[30]

I have estimated above that there are over 166,000 anti-Masonic videos on YouTube as of this date—and more are being uploaded every day. We need not be concerned about too many similar-looking comments showing up on many of them.

Rather, what we need to be concerned about is making a response to reach the great number of would-be Petitioners who look at these videos in an honest attempt to learn about the Fraternity.

---

[30] Within a year or so of the publication of this book, I hope to have release *Responding to Anti-Masonry: Guidelines for Rebutting the Top Twenty Anti-Masonic Claims Most-Frequently Encountered on the Internet*, which will include three-sentence comments suitable for the comment section on YouTube. Grand Lodges would be welcome to consult those in putting together their Recommended Responses documents.

Conclusion

We have been on quite a journey.

We have learned, on the one hand, that if we do not change what we are doing, if we just stay with business as usual, if we simply maintain the status quo—then Freemasonry is headed for virtual extinction within the lifetimes of the men whom we are now initiating.

On the other hand, we have learned that the causes for this distress are not mysterious. There are five specific problems that lead to the membership crisis in Freemasonry.

Finally, we have learned that there are five tasks that we can put our effort into to turn this situation around. The tasks are broadly defined, there are many sub-tasks, and there is something for every Mason to do: rank-and-file members, Lodge officers, RW DDGMs, and the MW Grand Master himself.

Along the way, I have observed that if we had initiated merely 5% of the adult male American population—a far lower proportion of than population than were Masons during the membership peaks after the two world wars—we would have upwards of 5 million American Masons. Today.

And we need those 5 million-plus Freemasons, brethren. We need them to fulfill the Masonic mission, part of which involves actually improving the society in which we live. We cannot hope to accomplish much even now, when we comprise one eligible man out of one hundred. We will have to give up any hope of accomplishing that part of our mission a generation or two from now, when we will be lucky to comprise one man out of 300, which is where we are headed under the status quo.

But one man out of twenty: as I said earlier, that constitutes a vanguard, a leading edge, a group that can make a difference in improving our society and our world.

Let us make this be so. Amen.

Appendix A

Masonic Membership Statistics, 1924-2016

In order to gain better control over where we are going, it helps to have a good idea of where we have been. In Appendix A, I present the membership statistics for American Freemasonry as reported by the Masonic Service Association, for the years 1924 (the earliest years for which figures are available) through 2016 (the latest year for which figures are available at this writing). I have added figures for the percent change in U.S. Masonic membership from the previous year.

For context, I also present annual figures for the population of the United States. Using these figures, and two guiding assumptions (that half the population is male, and that about 65% of the male population is of an appropriate age, 20 to 74 years old, to petition Freemasonry), I was able to estimate the number of American adult males in any given year. In turn, all these figures allowed me to calculate the proportion of American adult males who were Masons in any given year.

Source data for the population and membership figures, as well as the formulas for calculations, are given following the table.

I comment on the meaning and implications of these historical data following the table.

Table A-1.
U.S. Population and Masonic Membership, 1924-2016.

Year	U.S. Population	U.S. Adult Males	U.S. Masons	Mas. % Change from Previous Year	Masons as % of U.S. Adult Males
1924	114,109,000	37,085,425	3,077,161	N/A	8.30%
1925	115,829,000	37,644,425	3,157,566	+2.6%	8.39%
1926	117,397,000	38,154,025	3,218,375	+1.9%	8.44%
1927	119,035,000	38,686,375	3,267,241	+1.5%	8.45%
1928	120,509,000	39,165,425	3,295,872	+0.9%	8.42%
1929	121,767,000	39,574,275	3,295,125	+0.0%	8.33%
1930	123,076,741	39,999,941	3,279,778	-0.5%	8.20%
1931	124,039,648	40,312,886	3,216,307	-1.9%	7.98%
1932	124,840,471	40,573,153	3,069,645	-4.6%	7.57%
1933	125,578,763	40,813,098	2,901,758	-5.5%	7.11%
1934	126,373,773	41,071,476	2,760,451	-4.9%	6.72%
1935	127,250,232	41,356,325	2,659,218	-3.7%	6.43%
1936	128,053,180	41,617,284	2,591,309	-2.6%	6.23%
1937	128,824,829	41,868,069	2,549,772	-1.6%	6.09%
1938	129,824,939	42,193,105	2,514,595	-1.4%	5.96%
1939	130,879,718	42,535,908	2,482,291	-1.3%	5.84%
1940	132,122,446	42,939,795	2,457,263	-1.0%	5.72%
1941	133,402,471	43,355,803	2,451,301	-0.2%	5.65%
1942	134,859,553	43,829,355	2,478,892	+1.1%	5.66%
1943	136,739,353	44,440,290	2,561,844	+3.3%	5.76%
1944	138,397,345	44,979,137	2,719,607	+6.2%	6.05%
1945	139,928,165	45,476,654	2,896,343	+6.5%	6.37%
1946	141,388,566	45,951,284	3,097,713	+7.0%	6.74%
1947	144,126,071	46,840,973	3,281,371	+5.9%	7.01%
1948	146,631,302	47,655,173	3,426,155	+4.4%	7.19%
1949	149,188,130	48,486,142	3,545,757	+3.5%	7.31%

Table A-1 (continued).
U.S. Population and Masonic Membership, 1924-2016.

Year	U.S. Population	U.S. Adult Males	U.S. Masons	Mas. % Change from Previous Year	Masons as % of U.S. Adult Males
1950	152,271,417	49,488,211	3,644,634	+2.8%	7.36%
1951	154,877,889	50,335,314	3,726,744	+2.3%	7.40%
1952	157,552,740	51,204,641	3,808,364	+2.2%	7.44%
1953	160,184,192	52,059,862	3,893,350	+2.2%	7.48%
1954	163,025,854	52,983,403	3,964,118	+1.8%	7.48%
1955	165,931,202	53,927,641	4,009,925	+1.2%	7.44%
1956	168,903,031	54,893,485	4,053,323	+1.1%	7.38%
1957	171,984,130	55,894,842	4,085,676	+0.8%	7.31%
1958	174,881,904	56,836,619	4,099,928	+0.3%	7.21%
1959	177,829,628	57,794,629	4,103,161	+0.1%	7.10%
1960	180,671,158	58,718,126	4,099,219	-0.1%	6.98%
1961	183,691,481	59,699,731	4,086,499	-0.3%	6.85%
1962	186,537,737	60,624,765	4,063,563	-0.6%	6.70%
1963	189,241,798	61,503,584	4,034,020	-0.7%	6.56%
1964	191,888,791	62,363,857	4,005,605	-0.7%	6.42%
1965	194,302,963	63,148,463	3,987,690	-0.4%	6.31%
1966	196,560,338	63,882,110	3,948,193	-1.0%	6.18%
1967	198,712,056	64,581,418	3,910,509	-1.0%	6.06%
1968	200,706,052	65,229,467	3,868,854	-1.1%	5.93%
1969	202,676,946	65,870,007	3,817,846	-1.3%	5.80%
1970	205,052,174	66,641,957	3,763,213	-1.4%	5.65%
1971	207,660,677	67,489,720	3,718,718	-1.2%	5.51%
1972	209,896,021	68,216,207	3,661,507	-1.5%	5.37%
1973	211,908,788	68,870,356	3,611,448	-1.4%	5.24%
1974	213,853,928	69,502,527	3,561,767	-1.4%	5.12%
1975	215,973,199	70,191,290	3,512,628	-1.4%	5.00%

Table A-1 (continued).
U.S. Population and Masonic Membership, 1924-2016.

Year	U.S. Population	U.S. Adult Males	U.S. Masons	Mas. % Change from Previous Year	Masons as % of U.S. Adult Males
1976	218,035,164	70,861,428	3,470,980	-1.2%	4.90%
1977	220,239,425	71,577,813	3,418,844	-1.5%	4.78%
1978	222,584,545	72,339,977	3,360,409	-1.7%	4.65%
1979	225,055,487	73,143,033	3,304,334	-1.7%	4.52%
1980	227,224,681	73,848,021	3,251,528	-1.6%	4.40%
1981	229,465,714	74,576,357	3,188,175	-1.9%	4.28%
1982	231,664,458	75,290,949	3,121,746	-2.1%	4.15%
1983	233,791,994	75,982,398	3,060,242	-2.0%	4.03%
1984	235,824,902	76,643,093	2,992,389	-2.2%	3.90%
1985	237,923,795	77,325,233	2,914,421	-2.6%	3.77%
1986	240,132,887	78,043,188	2,839,962	-2.6%	3.64%
1987	242,288,918	78,743,898	2,763,828	-2.7%	3.51%
1988	244,498,982	79,462,169	2,682,537	-2.9%	3.38%
1989	246,819,230	80,216,250	2,608,935	-2.7%	3.25%
1990	249,622,814	81,127,415	2,531,643	-3.0%	3.12%
1991	252,980,941	82,218,806	2,452,676	-3.1%	2.98%
1992	256,514,224	83,367,123	2,371,863	-3.3%	2.85%
1993	259,918,588	84,473,541	2,293,949	-3.3%	2.72%
1994	263,125,821	85,515,892	2,225,611	-3.0%	2.60%
1995	266,278,393	86,540,478	2,153,316	-3.2%	2.49%
1996	269,394,284	87,553,142	2,089,578	-3.0%	2.39%
1997	272,646,925	88,610,251	2,021,909	-3.2%	2.28%
1998	275,854,104	89,652,584	1,967,208	-2.7%	2.19%
1999	279,040,168	90,688,055	1,902,588	-3.3%	2.10%
2000	282,162,411	91,702,784	1,841,169	-3.2%	2.01%
2001	284,968,955	92,614,910	1,774,200	-3.6%	1.92%

Table A-1 (continued).
U.S. Population and Masonic Membership, 1924-2016.

Year	U.S. Population	U.S. Adult Males	U.S. Masons	Mas. % Change from Previous Year	Masons as % of U.S. Adult Males
2002	287,625,193	93,478,188	1,727,505	-2.6%	1.85%
2003	290,107,933	94,285,078	1,671,255	-3.3%	1.77%
2004	292,805,298	95,161,722	1,617,032	-3.2%	1.70%
2005	295,516,599	96,042,895	1,569,812	-2.9%	1.63%
2006	298,379,912	96,973,471	1,525,131	-2.8%	1.57%
2007	301,231,207	97,900,142	1,483,449	-2.7%	1.52%
2008	304,093,966	98,830,539	1,444,823	-2.6%	1.46%
2009	306,771,529	99,700,747	1,404,059	-2.8%	1.41%
2010	309,338,421	100,534,987	1,373,453	-2.2%	1.37%
2011	311,644,280	101,284,391	1,336,503	-2.7%	1.32%
2012	313,993,272	102,047,813	1,306,539	-2.2%	1.28%
2013	316,234,505	102,776,214	1,246,241	-4.6%	1.21%
2014	318,622,525	103,552,321	1,211,183	-2.8%	1.17%
2015	321,039,839	104,337,948	1,157,987	-4.4%	1.11%
2016	323,405,935	105,106,929	1,117,781	-3.5%	1.06%

Note: All U.S. population figures are given as of July 1st of the year indicated. All U.S. Masonic membership figures are given as of December 31st of the year noted.

Data Sources

U.S. Population:

- 1924-1989: U. S. Census Bureau (2000).

- 1990-1999: U. S. Census Bureau (2002).

- 2000-2009: U. S. Census Bureau (2011).

- 2010-2016: U. S. Census Bureau (2017)

U.S. Masons: Figures reported by the Masonic Service Association of North America (n.d. [ca. 2017]).

Calculations

U.S. Adult Males: Calculated as follows. The number of U.S. Adult Males equals the U.S. Population, times 50% (the proportion of males in population), times 65% (the approximate proportion of the male population between the ages of 20 and 74).

Mas. % Change from Previous Year: Calculated as follows, for any given Year X. The Percent Change in the number of Masons from the Previous Year equals [the number of U.S. Masons for Year X, minus the number of U.S. Masons for the preceding year] divided by the number of U.S. Masons for the preceding year.

Masons as % of U.S. Adult Males: Calculated as follows. The number of Masons as a percentage of U.S. Adult Males equals the number of U.S. Masons divided by the number of U.S. Adult Males.

Observations on Masonic Membership

The year when we see the lowest Masonic membership in the United States is the latest year for which figures are available: 2016—essentially, the present. (Personally, it is a grating frustration to see the lowest Masonic membership occur at the same time that the population of the United States is at its highest.)

As it has often been noted, the highest U.S. Masonic membership occurred in 1959. However, as pointed out by

Belton (2001), this figure can be misleading as a measure of the strength or degree of popular acceptance of the Fraternity.

A better figure for measuring the relative strength of Freemasonry is not the *raw membership* figure, but rather the *proportion* of adult males who are Freemasons. By that measure, the strength of the Fraternity had already been declining since 1953, when the proportion of male adults who were Freemasons was 7.48%; by 1959, this proportion had declined by 7.1%, and as of 2016, it had declined to an abysmal 1.06%.

Yet even the 1953 high proportion of adult males who were Masons was only a *relative* peak. In the years for which figures are available, the highest proportions occurred in the 1920s. The *absolute* peak occurred in **1927**, when 8.45% of all American adult males were Freemasons—slightly more than 1 out of every 12 adult males.

Appendix B

Preparing and Conducting
a Chamber of Reflection

There are several fundamentals to understand about conducting a Chamber of Reflection: its purpose, how to prepare the space, and how to work with the Candidate. I describe each of these below. But first, allow me to explain my approach, which combines an appreciation for tradition with a desire to benefit the 21st-century Candidate.

A Modern Approach to the Chamber of Reflection

The history of the Chamber of Reflection is not well understood. It apparently dates back to the mid-18th century, perhaps no more than 40 years or so after the founding of the first Grand Lodge in 1717. The practice seems to have originated in France, and has long been associated with Continental Masonry—the Freemasonry of mainland Europe and its colonies in the New World—rather than with Freemasonry as practiced in Britain and its colonies in North America.

Continental Masonic ritual was heavily influenced by the original Scottish Rite. Despite its name, the earliest Scots Mason degree originally appeared in London about 1733, whence it spread to France and developed into the Scottish Rite; in France, even the first three Craft degrees were conducted according to the original Scottish Rite, and even to this day, the

Scottish Rite Craft degrees are worked in more countries than any other form of the Craft degrees.[31]

The rituals of Masonry on the Continent, under the influence of the original Scottish Rite. were much more overtly connected to the traditions of alchemy than the ceremonies of British Masonry. But even in Britain, it is thought, one of the reasons for the founding of Speculative Freemasonry was to give learned men an opportunity to discuss esoteric subjects, such as alchemy and kabbalah, in the privacy that was available within the walls of a tyled lodge room. (Of course, Masonry was established in Britain and France at a time when the open discussion of esoteric topics could create problems between the esotericist and either State, Church, or both.)

Because many Freemasons in 17th- and 18th-century Britain and France seem to have had strong interests in alchemy, we should not be surprised if Candidates of that day were generally better acquainted with alchemical symbolism and language than are American candidates in the 21st century. This difference has consequences.

Of course, in 18th-century Britain and France, an alchemically minded Candidate would know that the rooster is an alchemical symbol of the substance mercury. Of course, he would know that mercury was one of the *tria prima*, the "three primes" of which all material substances were composed, the other two being salt and sulfur. Of course, he would know that alchemy is in part concerned with the discovery or crea-

---

[31]   de Hoyos (2018). I eagerly await the forthcoming book being written by Arturo de Hoyos and Josef Wages, which will present more evidence regarding the development of the Scottish Rite rituals than has ever been published before.

tion of the Philosopher's Stone, so he would understand an alchemical motto like "visit the interior of the earth, and, purifying it, you will find the hidden stone," as well as this motto's Latin acronym, V.I.T.R.I.O.L. (because, of course, he knew Latin as well as his native language). Of course, he would understand that alchemical knowledge was meant to be applied to the task, not just of the transformation of materials, but to the transformation of oneself, as well.

And, of course, what was clear to the 18th-century European Candidate is completely unknown material to most 21st-century American Candidates.

So, what are we to do? On the one hand, the Chamber of Reflection experience can be powerful in orienting the Candidate to his initiation as the beginning of a personal transformation. On the other hand, the typical modern Candidate does not have the background to benefit from the Chamber symbolism when conducted in the classic Continental style.

The solution that I have chosen is to make some adjustments to the symbolism presented in the Chamber of Reflection. For example, the rooster is gone. I have also added some explanations and questions meant to provoke reflection. I leave it to the reader to study, ponder, and decide whether my Recommendations would improve the experience for the 21st-century American candidate.

The Purpose of the Chamber of Reflection

The ultimate purpose of the Chamber of Reflection experience is to put Candidates in an appropriate frame of mind in which to receive the mysteries of Freemasonry through a degree ceremony to follow. This purpose has nothing to do with scaring Candidates—although, in our superficial and materialistic popular culture, some Candidates may indeed be shaken by being confronted so directly with the thought of their own mortality and transformation, and by injunctions to consider a greater perspective on their lives. This is entirely a good thing.

It is important to understand that the power of the Chamber of Reflection lies in the *intention* that the experience evokes in the Candidate—not in any object or objects. **The objective of the experience is to evoke in the Candidate the intention to enter into Masonic initiation as the beginning of a profound personal transformation.** Everything in the experience—the symbols of mortality, the mirror, the alchemical mottos, and more—are in the service of that objective.

Consequently, the *only* indispensable objects needed for the experience are a quiet space, a table, a chair, some paper, and a pen. Success is found in doing the best we can with the materials, resources, and personnel that we have at hand.

To fulfill its objective, the Chamber of Reflection involves three types of things. The most obvious are the *symbols and mottos* of mortality, and of wisdom. The experience also involves *actions* on the part of the Candidate, to encourage reflection. Finally, a *Conductor* leads the Candidates through the experience.

Preparing the Space for a Chamber of Reflection

Preparing the space for a Chamber of Reflection involves providing a place for the Chamber itself, and preparing the symbolism and mottos.

The Chamber Itself

In the classic style, a Chamber of Reflection is conducted in a room dedicated for this purpose. The walls of the Chamber are painted black, and various symbols and mottos are painted on these black walls in stark white paint.

However, today's reality is that many lodges do not have a room to dedicate to a Chamber of Reflection. Each lodge must conduct the Chamber in a way that works for that lodge's circumstances. Here are some recommendations:

- Explore the possibility that a room may be available in the lodge building. It is not necessary for the Chamber to be right next to, or even near, either the lodge room or the room where candidates are prepared for initiation. The room may be anywhere in the building. I have heard about one lodge that converted a large broom closet to a dedicated Chamber of Reflection; this lodge only initiated one Candidate at a time, and in this circumstance, not much space was required.

- In some cities, several lodges meet within a building that has multiple lodge rooms. In this circumstance, it may be possible to find a single, smaller room within the building that can be made over into a dedicated Chamber of Reflection, which is then shared by the various lodges who meet there. This would require a bit of scheduling, but it would be worth it. If the Chamber can accommodate several Candidates at one time, there is no reason why Candidates from different lodges might not share the experience, if they are to be initiated on the same evening.

- Many a lodge has one multi-purpose room (basically a small conference room) in the lodge building. Such a room can be converted efficiently and quickly into a temporary but workable Chamber of Reflection. With a little work, one can drape the walls with black curtains. In advance, one either paints the symbols and mottos in white directly on the curtains, or one prepares black placards (from construction paper, perhaps) with the symbols and mottos painted in white; the placards are then hung onto the black curtains.

- A variation of this idea involves the dining area that many lodges have within their building. To create a temporary Chamber of Reflection, one could create "walls" by stringing up black curtains around a portion of the dining area. The symbols might be hung from the curtains on the kind of placards that I have described earlier.

- Some lodges rent out a single room within a commercial building in which to hold lodge. In such circumstances, one might use black curtains to 'wall off' a section of the foyer or hallway in front of the lodge room to use as the Chamber of Reflection, much as I have described above for the use of the dining area.

As an example of this last idea used in a creative way, I am thinking of a lodge I have heard of that met in an upper floor of a small business building that was otherwise unused on the weekends. This lodge used the *elevator*, decorated and furnished appropriately, as a Chamber of Reflection! Truly, this suggests that where there is a will, there is a way.

Preparing the Practical and Symbolic Objects, Written Symbols, and Mottos

The Chamber of Reflection traditionally involves the use of a few practical and symbolic objects, as well as written mottos painted in white on the curtains or walls of the Chamber.

The Practical Objects

Table and Chair(s)

The Chamber must include a table to use as a writing surface; the table must also be able to accommodate a few other practical and symbolic objects (described below). The Chamber must also contain a chair for each Candidate.

Light Source

The Chamber requires lighting; light of a low level is preferred. A candle or three would be ideal if fire regulations permit; otherwise, use a table lamp with a low-watt bulb.

Writing Paper and a Pen

Each Candidate will require writing paper and a pen.

Card of Instructions

The table should have on it a Card of Instructions for each Candidate; quality card stock is a plus. The Card of Instructions has on it such material as the following:

READ THIS IMMEDIATELY!

INSTRUCTIONS FOR THE CHAMBER OF REFLECTION

You are here to reflect upon your life, and how Freemasonry is about to change it.

Do not speak to anyone else within the Chamber except your Conductor.

Consider each of the symbols placed upon the table and drawn upon the wall. Consider the interpretation of each of these symbols on the accompanying Explanation of Symbolism.

Meditate upon these symbols.

Using the paper and pen provided, write your name and the date, and answer these questions:

1. What is your duty to the Supreme Being?

2. What is your duty to your fellow human beings?

3. What is your duty to yourself?

Your Conductor will come for you at the conclusion of your time here. Leave your papers behind. They shall be held unread at the Lodge and given to you at the conclusion of the Third Degree (or earlier if you do not proceed).

{To use when only *one Candidate is present, and a full-length mirror is placed on the wall behind his chair, out of his sight:}* It is not always before oneself that one finds his enemies. That which is to be feared the most is many times behind oneself. Turn around!

Card of Explanation of Symbolism

The table should have on it a Card of Explanation of Symbolism for each Candidate. This card has on it such material as the following:

EXPLANATION OF SELECTED SYMBOLISM

THE CHAMBER: This darkened room is symbolic of three things: a Cave for reflection and meditation; the Grave; the Womb. These are related.

THE SKULL: A symbol of mortality. Death can occur on more than one level. Traditionally, death is a prelude to coming forth into a new life.

THE HOURGLASS: A symbol of the brevity of life.

V.I.T.R.I.O.L.: The word *vitriol* was used in alchemy to denote what we now call sulfuric acid, a powerful and dangerous substance that, when used carefully, is important in breaking down, refining, and synthesizing materials. The initials *V.I.T.R.I.O.L.* stand for the words of a Latin alchemical motto which, translated into English, states "visit the interior of the earth, and, purifying it, you will find the hidden stone."

MAGNUM OPUS: Latin for "(The) Great Work." In alchemy, this is the work of creating the Philosopher's Stone—which could turn that which was base and crude into that which was perfect.

Ask yourself: why do we present these symbols and mottos to you?

The Symbolic Objects

The Skull

A skull (with or without a jawbone; crossbones optional) is placed on the table.

The Hourglass

An hourglass is placed on the table. (Preferably this is full-sized, that is, it holds a full hour's worth of sand. Of course, we work with what we have.) Alternatively, this may be painted on the walls or curtains of the Chamber.

The Sickle

A large sickle, of the kind used to harvest wheat, should be in a corner of the Chamber. Alternatively, this may be painted on the walls or curtains of the Chamber.

Mirror

The Mirror is to be used only when just a single Candidate is presented to the Chamber. In that case, a full-length mirror should be placed behind the Candidate's chair, so that when he is seated, he cannot see it unless he turns around.

The Mottos

The following mottos should be painted on the walls, curtains, or placards hung on the walls or curtains of the Chamber:

- V.I.T.R.I.O.L.
- Magnum Opus

- Our gold is not the common gold.

- Know Thyself.

- Ponder, then decide—to proceed, or to withdraw.

- Symbolism yields only to *perseverance*.
  Its lessons must be pursued with *vigilance*.

- If your soul is frightened, do not continue.

- If curiosity brought you here, leave!

- If you are capable of deception, tremble: you will be found out.

- If you take care about differences or distinctions amongst people, leave: we do not know them here.

- Seek not here for reputation or the outer wealth.

Working with the Candidate

Before the Candidate(s) arrive, the following tasks should be completed:

- The Card of Instruction should be placed on the table at the place where the Candidate will sit. The Card of Explanation of Symbolism should be underneath it.

- The writing paper should be placed to one side of the Cards.

- A working pen should be placed on top of the writing paper.

- The candle(s), if any, should be lit.

The member of the lodge assigned as the Conductor meets with the Candidate(s) and places a blindfold on him or them. (It would be helpful for the Conductor to have an assistant or two, so that there is one member of the lodge to conduct each Candidate.)

If there is just one Candidate, the Conductor places him in a chair facing the table, with the mirror to the Candidate's back. (If there is more than one Candidate, it may be wise not to use the Mirror. In this case, the Cards of Instructions given to the Candidate should not have the paragraph involving the Mirror.)

The Conductor says the following to the Candidate:

- "Remove your blindfold."

- (If other Candidates are present:) "Do not speak to one another. Speak to no one but me when you are in this room."

- "You will be here for one hour {or whatever time period has been allotted by the lodge]. Use your time well."

- (Optional:) If a full hourglass is on the table, *and* if the experience is to last a full hour, the Conductor turns the hourglass over so that the full side is at the top, preferably with a loud >THUNK<, like the sound of a gavel.

- "There is a Card of Instructions before you. Read it!"

The Conductor leaves the Candidate(s). At the conclusion of the experience, the Conductor does the following:

- The Conductor enters the room and directs the Candidate(s) to leave their papers and exit the room. (If there is more than one Candidate, the Conductor admonishes them to keep silence.)

- The Conductor places whatever the Candidate has written in a file folder with the Candidate's name on it, to be delivered to the Candidate at the conclusion of his Master Mason degree (or his prior withdrawal); the Conductor keeps this folder to put it in the safe-keeping of the Secretary.

- **The Conductor blows out the lit candles, if any have been used.**

- The Conductor allows the Candidate(s) to use the lavatory, if necessary, but admonishes the Candidate(s) to do so in silence.

- When all are ready, the Conductor brings the Candidate(s) to the Preparation Room, and puts them in the custody of the Senior Deacon.

- If he has not already done so, the Conductor delivers Candidates' papers to the Secretary.

Once or Thrice?

One open question is the matter of how many times the Candidate should be given the Chamber of Reflection experience. Some would say that the Candidate should receive this experience once, before the initiation as Entered Apprentice. Others would say that the Candidate should have this opportunity before each of the three Craft Degrees.

Lodges differ greatly in their resources. My own opinion is that if a lodge has the resources and personnel to do so, the Candidate would benefit from having the opportunity to engage in the Chamber of Reflection experience before each Degree. Especially if the lodge follows my advice, given above (Rec. #8), that there should be intervals of six to twelve months between degrees, the Candidate will come to each Chamber of Reflection with different levels of maturity and insight. In a real sense, this creates three different Chamber of Reflection experiences, rather than the same experience three times.

Resources

Those who wish to learn more about the Chamber of Reflection as conducted in the classic style may consult various online articles ("Chamber of Reflection," 2017; Da Costa, 1999/2001; Livingstone, 2014; Lombardo, 2006; Martinez, 2009; Stavish, 2002). Some of this material has been presented in an online video (Stewart, 2016).

Appendix C

Conducting a
Master Mason Rededication Ceremony

The typical "Masonic rededication" is the rededication of a lodge *building*. That is a completely different matter than the subject under consideration, the Master Mason Rededication Ceremony, which involves a lodge's Master Masons rededicating *themselves* through symbolically renewing the Obligations, and receiving the Charges, of each of the Three Degrees.

There are different ways to arrange personnel for this event. One may conduct this ceremony using only the officers of the lodge. Alternatively, one may add the involvement of a District Lecturer or District Deputy Grand Master, which does add something special to the event.

The lodge is opened as usual. All business except dealing with urgent needs is deferred to the next meeting, and the ceremony itself is the designated Masonic education of the evening. No one is admitted, and the Tyler does not even knock at the door, during the Ceremony.

There are a dozen sequential actions involved in conducting this ceremony (some of them very brief). I describe these below. Having the ceremony itself proceed smoothly and from memory adds to the impact of the event; a rehearsal is likely in order.

1. Present opening remarks.

The Worshipful Master welcomes the brethren to the event.

2. Direct the brethren in how to present themselves before the altar for the First Degree rededication.

The Worshipful Master directs one to three Exemplars to kneel at the West of the Altar. Except for the person leading the First Obligation (see below), the brethren present assemble themselves behind the kneeling Exemplars. One or two brethren lay a hand on a shoulder of each Exemplar; more brethren each lay a hand on the shoulder of each of *those* brethren, and so on, until all these brethren are connected physically in chains that begin at the Exemplar(s). (Which hand is to be placed on a brother's shoulder depends on the Degree being given.)

3. Direct the brethren in reciting the Obligation of the First Degree.

A designated brother, standing East of the altar, leads the entire lodge through a recitation of the Obligation of the First Degree. At the end of the Obligation, he then directs the brethren to drop hands, and tells the Exemplars that they may stand.

4. Deliver the Charge of the First Degree.

A designated brother then delivers the Charge of the First Degree to the assembled brethren from the podium or the steps of the dais.

5. Direct the brethren in how to present themselves before the altar for the Second Degree rededication.

A designated brother directs one to three Exemplars to kneel at the West of the Altar. (Select different Exemplars than were used before!) Except for the person leading the Obligation, the brethren assemble themselves behind the kneeling Exemplars, hands on shoulders as before.

6. Direct the brethren in reciting the Obligation of the Second Degree.

A designated brother, standing East of the altar, leads the entire lodge through a recitation of the Obligation of the Second Degree. At the end of the Obligation, he then directs the brethren to drop hands, and tells the Exemplars that they may stand.

7. Deliver the Charge of the Second Degree.

A designated brother delivers the Charge of the Second Degree to the assembled brethren from the podium or the steps of the dais.

8. Direct the brethren in how to present themselves before the altar for the Third Degree rededication.

A designated brother directs one to three Exemplars to kneel at the West of the Altar (again, selecting different Exemplars than were used before). Except for the person leading the Obligation, the brethren assemble themselves behind the kneeling Exemplars, hands on shoulders as before.

9. Direct the brethren in reciting the Obligation of the Third Degree.

A designated brother, standing East of the altar, leads the entire lodge through a recitation of the Obligation of the Third Degree. At the end of the Obligation, he then directs the brethren to drop hands, and tells the Exemplars that they may stand.

10. Deliver the Charge of the Third Degree.

A designated brother delivers the Charge of the Third Degree to the assembled brethren from the podium or the steps of the dais.

This brother then invites all present to take their regular seats in the lodge.

11. Make closing remarks.

The Worshipful Master or visiting dignitary delivers closing remarks on the occasion.

12. Invitation to offer personal reactions.

The person delivering the closing remarks invites those present to share their reactions to the experience of Masonic rededication. Up to three brethren or so give their reactions. (This step may switch places with Step #11.)

After the ceremony, the lodge is closed in the usual fashion.

Appendix D

Instructing Candidates in the Preparation of a Masonic Research Paper

The term "Masonic research paper" seems portentous and heavy, something that conjures up images of bound volumes of the *Ars Quatuor Coronatorum* (the published transactions of the premier lodge of research, Quatuor Coronati Lodge No. 2076 in London). Brethren, it simply does not have to be so hard.

There are four things for Candidates to know when it comes to preparing a Masonic research paper:

1. how to approach the task

2. how to select a topic

3. where to find information about the topic

4. how to structure and write the paper itself.

In instructing Candidates, it may be helpful to frame the task in terms of these four issues, which I address below.

How to Approach the Task

Candidates need to understand that the task at hand is a very limited one, and can be completed without too much pain by anyone who has survived a couple of years of high school. We are looking for a very basic, entry-level Masonic research paper, not a ground-breaking piece of scholarship (although original thought is appreciated), of about five typed pages in length, plus references. The objectives of the paper are to show that (1) the Candidate has thought hard about some aspect of the symbolism or philosophy of Freemasonry, (2) the Candidate can use reliable sources about Freemasonry, and (3) the Candidate can apply this aspect of Masonic symbolism or philosophy to his life. If the Candidate demonstrates this, then the assignment is completed in acceptable form.

How to Select a Topic

The Candidate should select as a topic the symbolism and philosophy of Freemasonry as shown in the Degree that the Candidate has most recently received. This might include:

- the working tools of the Degree

- the different aspects of the Degree ritual (given that 'ritual is symbolism acted out')

- the visual symbols displayed in the Lodge Room or illustrated on the Tracing Board of the Degree

- the philosophical or moral precepts mentioned in the ritual or the Lecture of the Degree.

Where to Find Information About the Topic

There is an immense amount of information available in print and online regarding Freemasonry. Unfortunately, a large proportion of this information is useless, given that it ranges along a spectrum from simply uninformed and inaccurate to downright delusional. Part of the point of this task is to help the Candidate learn about responsible sources of information about Freemasonry.

Lodges differ greatly in their on-site resources of Masonic information. Some lodges have modest book rooms or shelves within the lodge building itself. Some lodges are located with several other lodges in a large Masonic building that features a full-scale library of Masonic materials. Other lodges have nothing in the way of Masonic literature in the lodge building.

In addition, many communities have public libraries with books on Freemasonry, some of which are in the reliable category. Finally, it should be pointed out that many of the classic reliable works on Freemasonry (such as Mackey's *Symbolism of Freemasonry*) are available at no cost online. As in so many other areas of life, here too, we do the best we can with what we have where we are.

Candidates should avail themselves—either from lodge or Grand Lodge libraries, public libraries, or online sources, of books such as the following which address Masonic symbolism in a responsible way, suitable for a beginner:

- Albert G. Mackey, *The Symbolism of Freemasonry*. Originally published in 1869, this book is widely available in reprint and online editions.[32]

- Albert G. Mackey, *Lexicon of Freemasonry*. Originally published in 1845, this book is widely available in reprint and online editions.[33]

---

[32] Mackey's *The Symbolism of Freemasonry* is available online for free: https://www.gutenberg.org/files/11937/11937-h/11937-h.htm

[33] Mackey's *Lexicon of Freemasonry* is available for free online: https://archive.org/details/alexiconfreemas00mackgoog

- Robert Macoy, *A Dictionary of Freemasonry: A History, Encyclopedia, and Dictionary*. Originally published 1868-1870, this book is widely available in reprint and online editions.[34]

Although there are other excellent books that one might recommend (such as Roberts' *The Craft and Its Symbols*, and several books by W. Kirk MacNulty), several of these have the disadvantage of presenting symbols divided up under the heading of each Degree. I believe there is some advantage to presenting the symbolism to Candidates one Degree at a time, and so I am not recommending these books for the purpose of Candidates preparing their papers.

How to Structure and Write the Paper Itself

The paper should be written *as if* it were to be delivered orally in a tyled lodge composed of Masons who had attained the Candidate's degree or higher. As such, although the Candidate may not quote the ritual openly in writing (which would be a violation of his Obligation), the Candidate may leave spaces to indicate where he would quote the ritual if he were delivering the paper orally in lodge.

The paper that the Candidate prepares should be structured in five parts, each of which I describe below:

1. Introduction

2. Meaning

3. Application

---

[34] Macoy's *A Dictionary of Freemasonry* is available for free online: https://archive.org/details/generalhistorycy00macoiala

4. Reflection

5. References

Introduction

In this part, the Candidate states what aspect of symbolism, ritual, or philosophy he will be addressing in his paper.

Meaning

Here, the candidate describes how the symbol, ritual action, or philosophical value comes up in the Degree ceremony, and what meaning is attached to it there.

The candidate then expands on the meaning and importance of this topic as it has been addressed by some of those who have written about Masonry over the years. (Of course, like the honest Mason he is, the Candidate uses quotation marks for direct quotations, and gives the appropriate citations—such as "Mackey, 1845, p. 216"—for both direct quotations and indirect quotations.)

Application

This is the heart of the paper. In this section, the Candidate applies the meaning of the symbol, ritual act, or philosophical value to the life of a Mason.

This application can show up in a Mason's life in various ways. For example, it might affect the way that the Mason treats his spouse or significant other. It may affect the way that the Mason interacts with his children, or members of his extended family. It may affect the way he acts with his neighbors, or the way he relates to his religious or spiritual community. It may affect the way he deals with co-workers or customers at work; it may have an impact on the way he deals with students or teachers at school.

Keep in mind that inner changes—if indeed they are real—manifest themselves externally in behavior. Perhaps the Mason is inspired to humility through a given aspect of the Degree ceremony. (I am sure that the initiated reader can think of aspects of any Degree ceremony that might inspire humility.) How might that humility be manifest in the Mason's life, work, or relationships with others?

The Candidate composes this part of the paper in the general case, that is, from the point of view of how the symbol, ritual act, or philosophical precept might affect the life of *any* Mason, in any number of circumstances. The next part of the paper becomes more personal.

Reflection

In this part, the Candidate reflects on how the symbol, ritual act, or philosophical precept might affect *his* life personally. One expects that the ideas reflected in the topic might suggest that the Candidate should change something in his life—maybe several things. What are some of those changes?

References

The Candidate should give reference information in simple form for anything that either provided a quotation or that inspired some thought that shows up in the paper. We need not obsess about reference/citation style.

What Happens With the Paper Next?

Every Candidate should deliver his paper before his Instructor and (if any) his fellow Candidates. This is a good way for him to resolve bashfulness about public speaking, and it will help develop his leadership capacity for his life as a Mason going forward.

Some lodges make it a practice to have their Candidates deliver their papers before the entire lodge, as part of Masonic education. There are some advantages to this practice. (For one, the lodge gets to know something about their Candidates through their selection of topic, the content of their paper, and their delivery.) However, I do not consider these advantages to be of paramount importance.

If the lodge is conducting Masonic education as I suggest it should (see Chapter 9), the lodge will have a well thought-out plan for what it will cover in Masonic education throughout the year—a plan devised with the needs of the lodge's members uppermost in mind. Having Candidates deliver their papers here and there throughout the year might interfere with this plan. For this reason, I do not recommend that Candidates' papers be delivered before the lodge as a matter of course.

Some lodges will wish to make time *both* for a Candidate to deliver his paper *and* for a full-length, regularly scheduled session of Masonic education. When possible, this might be the best policy to implement.

Appendix E

How to Prepare and Conduct a Masonic Open House

In Chapter 10 ("Build the Lighthouse: Tell the World About Freemasonry"), I suggest that each Particular Lodge and each Grand Lodge should hold Open Houses for the public, annually. (See Recommendations #25 and #29, in Chapter 9.) In this Appendix, I describe how to accomplish this.

Please note: What I describe below is an ideal description. Embrace the circumstances of your Lodge, and do what you can.

The Particular Lodge Open House

Below, I describe four things: what an Open House looks like; the preparation that goes into a quality Open House, organized by a timeline; the personnel required to conduct an Open House; and, an agenda for what goes on during the Open House itself.

1. What an Open House Looks Like

The Masonic Open House at a Particular Lodge features four types of activities: A formal welcome, informational displays, the delivery of a formal address, and a formal close.

A. The Formal Welcome

The Lodge building should be open at least half an hour before the announced beginning of the activity. At the announced beginning time, the appointed officer should welcome any visitors who have arrived, with a brief announcement that mentions the following:

- "We welcome you to the Open House of <name> Masonic Lodge Number __, Free and Accepted Masons in the State of __."[35] (Precision in this section is important; it alludes to the size of the organization, and subtly emphasizes that we are organized by state, not an overall national organization or international conspiracy.)

- Explain that there will be a formal address regarding the meaning and purpose of Freemasonry, delivered in the lodge room, at the appointed time. (As I explain below, I recommend that this address be delivered at least *twice*.)

- Explain that, throughout the event, there are informational displays for their perusal, along with Masons who will be glad to answer any questions they may have.

- Enjoy!

---

[35] Please adjust to local custom, for example, "Ancient Free and Accepted Masons," and so on. Brethren of the Prince Hall Affiliation should, of course, make the necessary adjustments to the name of their Jurisdiction.

Subsequent to the formal welcome, the brethren assigned as Greeters should mention this information to visitors as they arrive.

B. *The Informational Displays*

In Chapter 10, I described the Five Messages of the Masonic Open House, five points that we want the public to understand about Freemasonry. The first of these messages—the idea that the Masonic Fraternity not only still exists, but it meets in their community—is fulfilled simply by holding the Open House itself. The other four messages each should be described in its own informational display, as follows:

- "What Freemasonry Is." This display explains that Freemasonry is a fraternal society of adult men who are interested in improving their characters through symbolic and philosophical initiations and discussions.

- "What Freemasonry Is *Not*." This display explains that Freemasonry has nothing to do with the many rumors that people hear: Masonry is not a religion; Masonry is not concerned with world domination, mind control, or devil worship. (Yes, this may disappoint some visitors.)

- "How Men Become Freemasons." This display explains that there is a process that men can follow if they would like to become Freemasons, and lays out the steps in that process. Wording here is important in order to avoid recruitment. (So, obviously, no wording like "Become a Mason!")

- "Masonry, Women, and Youth." This display explains that there are local organizations affiliated with Freemasonry for women and for youth. This is where you will mention explicitly what opportunities exist for membership in the Order of the Eastern Star, the Order of the Amaranth, DeMolay, the Rainbow, the Triangles, and so forth. It is important to be explicit regarding (1) what these organizations do, (2) what the membership requirements are, and (3) how to learn more.

The displays could easily and inexpensively be created using the kind of display boards used for school science fairs.[36]

One important element that is often overlooked: Each display station should have photocopies of a ***one-sheet summary***, for visitors to take away with them. Even the minimal set-up that I describe above will present visitors with a great deal of information to digest; remember, at this point in the 21st century, the typical American starts off with little or no experience of or knowledge about serious fraternal organizations. Let us make it easy for visitors to retain the information to which they have been exposed.

Lodges with a lot of display space might want to have additional displays in addition to the basic displays I have mentioned above. These might include displays on the following topics:

---

[36]　Again, I suggest that the Lodge obtain relatively inexpensive boards, such as what is available here on Amazon: https://smile.amazon.com/Darice-36-Inch-by-48-Inch-Project-Display-Board/dp/B004GXBYTI/

- The values of Freemasonry (for example, the four Cardinal Virtues; the three Principal Tenets; the three Theological Virtues; egalitarianism; logic, science, and faith combined).

- "Is Freemasonry a Secret Society?" (I would point out that truly secret societies do not hold Open Houses!)

- "Freemasonry and Religion." (Keep in mind that substantial numbers of people believe that Freemasonry is a satanic religion engaged in devil worship; or, that it is Deism; or, that it teaches that all religions are equal; or, that it is at war, either with Christianity in general or Roman Catholicism in particular. People will need to be disabused of these notions. Note that **at no time** should any Lodge member at the Open House give his opinion about religious organizations, such as churches, or make a statement about what they teach, or why they teach what they teach about Freemasonry or anything else. You are presenting yourselves as experts about Freemasonry—period.)

- "Why are some things 'secret' in Freemasonry?"

- "What happens during a Masonic initiation?"

- "How did Freemasonry begin?" (One must be careful to distinguish the mythic history from the factual history.)

- Masonic charities.

C. *The Formal Address*

One might argue that the informational displays give a good overview and introduction to Freemasonry, and so a formal address is redundant. However, informational displays are, by their very nature, *visual*; the reality is that some people take in information much better by *auditory* means—basically, preferring to take in new information by hearing rather than by seeing—and we need to take this basic characteristic of human nature into account.

The formal address should be about 15-20 minutes long. There are different possible approaches that one can make to content here:

- "What Freemasonry Is and Is Not"

- "What Freemasonry Stands For" (that is, Masonic values)

- "What I Give to Freemasonry, and What I Get Back In Return"

Whatever approach one takes, one should always begin by welcoming the visitors, and always conclude by encouraging them to see the informational displays.

I strongly recommend that a formal address should be delivered every 90 minutes or so of the Open House. Some lodges will prefer to deliver the same address, while others will prefer different addresses at different times. Either way, it is important to recognize that any individual visitor is only likely to spend so much time at the Open House, and so there will be new visitors to attend to.

D. The Formal Close

At the conclusion of the allotted time, it is important to formally close the event. It would be sufficient to have an officer say, wherever the displays are set up, that it is time for the conclusion of the event, and that he and the lodge thank all who have attended.

2. Preparation and Timeline

Like any event, a Masonic Lodge Open House does not just "happen." The necessary planning and preparation are described below.

Beginning of the Masonic Year

The Lodge Open House should be placed in the Lodge calendar from the beginning of the year (or earlier, if the Lodge plans certain events more than one year out). Funds from the budget should be allocated at this time (see below).

At the time the Open House is placed on the calendar, one of the Officers or another member of the Lodge should be placed in charge of the event. He may delegate different responsibilities to others, and he may seek volunteers to help, but it is he who is in charge of the event, he who will give periodic reports to the Lodge regarding the status of preparations, and he who will report on this assignment to the Lodge following the event.

From the Beginning of the Masonic Year to Three Months Before the Open House

By a date three months before the Open House, the person in charge should have a crystal-clear idea of the following:

- how the space within the Lodge building will be allocated;

- regarding displays: where the displays will be, what displays will be shown, and who will be posted at the displays to answer inquiries (including changes of shift, if any);

- regarding formal presentations: who will be speaking, and what they will be speaking about.

Having this all squared away over three months ahead of time might seem excessive. I assure you that it is not. The last three months before an Open House have a tendency to slip away quickly; there will be changes in personnel due to changes in personal circumstances and personal emergencies. The farther out you make preparations, the easier it will be to make adjustments.

Three Months Before the Open House

Now is the time to start making displays, which should be completed no later than a full month before the Open House. Of course, content should be approved by the person in charge of the event and by the Worshipful Master.

Now would also be a great time for those assigned to deliver formal addresses to start real work on their presentations, which should be complete and shown to the assigned officer by a full month before the Open House. An Open House is not the time to discover that a brother giving a presentation has very unorthodox and controversial opinions about Freemasonry—opinions that he has no qualms about sharing with the general public. The officer in charge should vet all talks; at his discretion, so may the Worshipful Master.

One Month Before the Open House

The month before the Open House is all about publicity. Local print, radio, and television media should all be contacted no later than the month before the Open House. If posters are being printed, these should be put up in no later than two full weeks before the Open House.

3. Personnel Required

On the day of the event itself, there needs to be someone who has been assigned in advance to man each display. Assign people for multiple shifts; no one should be asked to man a display for longer than 45 minutes or so without a break. Well-staffed lodges may wish to have two brethren at each display. Additional personnel includes one or two greeters at the door of the Lodge building. I find that it is useful to have one or two members of the Lodge assigned to make sure, in a friendly way, that young visitors do not get into mischief.

The person in charge of the event itself should have no further official responsibilities than opening and closing the event, announcing the formal presentations, supervising the overall event, and lending a hand where necessary. This is "management by wandering around."[37]

4. Budget

Budget falls into three categories:

1. Displays.

---

[37] MBWA is an actual management style which has been quite successful in some business settings.

2. Food. Some lodges will wish to provide light re-freshments. **Note:** Provide ingredients for the snacks, to warn away people with food aller-gies—which can be fatal.

3. Posters. If lodges have the means, formal printed posters—of the type used to advertise benefits and carnivals—can be useful in advertising an event.

5. Agenda for the Event

Depending on the circumstances of a given Lodge, an Open House can last anywhere from two to six hours. A "deluxe" version might have an agenda like the following:

- Formal greeting
- Displays: Shift #1 (30-45 minutes)
- Formal Presentation #1 (15-20 minutes)
- Displays: Shift #2 (30-45 minutes)
- Formal Presentation #2 (15-20 minutes)
- <repeat as desired>
- Formal conclusion and farewell

The Grand Lodge Masonic Day

The purpose of the Grand Lodge Masonic Day is basically the same as that of a Particular Lodge's Open House. Howev-er, it is conducted on a grander scale, with more personnel, a larger budget, and perhaps more and better-produced dis-plays.

Some Grand Lodges are blessed with a Library, a Museum, or both, where display cases of historical artifacts and such can make the point that Freemasonry in this locale has been around for quite some time. Efforts should be made to have members of the local news media in attendance; the Grand Lodge Masonic Day is a perfect opportunity for the sort of "local color" story that is favored by local newspapers and the local news sections of regional or national newspapers, as well as local television stations, including affiliates of national networks. ("A day with the Masons: tape at eleven!")

Embrace this. Keep in mind that, as I have said earlier in this book, large swaths of the public either do not realize that Freemasonry still exists as a living tradition, or they have bizarre notions of what we are about. The Grand Lodge Masonic Day, especially if continued on an annual basis, can be an effective way to let the public know that we are here, and who we really are. After that, those who truly seek what we have to offer will take it upon themselves to find us.

References

Anderson, J. (1734). *The constitutions of the Free-Masons* [online edition]. Philadelphia, PA: Benjamin Franklin. (Original work published 1723). Consulted June 14, 2016 at http://digitalcommons.unl.edu/cgi/viewcontent.cgi?article=1028&context=libraryscience

Annual reports and financial statements for the period ending December 31, 2015. (2016, May). [New York, NY]: The Grand Lodge of Free and Accepted Masons in the State of New York. Available online at http://nymasons.org/2016/wp-content/uploads/2016-Officers-etc-Booklet-Blue-Cover.pdf (consulted June 4, 2016.

Bauer, A. (2007). *Isaac Newton's Freemasonry: The alchemy of science and mysticism.* Rochester, VT: Inner Traditions.

Belton, J. L. (2001). Masonic membership myths debunked. *Heredom: The Transactions of the Scottish Rite Research Society, 9,* 9-31.

Berger, P., Davie, G., & Foas, E. (2008). *Religious America, secular Europe? A theme and variations.* Burlington, VT: Ashgate.

Chamber of Reflection [online article]. (2017, May 20). *Wikipedia.* Consulted May 25, 2018 at https://en.wikipedia.org/wiki/Chamber_of_Reflection

Coil, H. W. (1996). *Coil's Masonic encyclopedia* (rev. ed., W. M. Brown, W. L. Cummings, H. Van Buren Voorhis, & A. E.

Roberts, Eds.). Richmond, VA: Macoy Publishing and Masonic Supply Co., Inc.

Covey, S. R. (1990). *The seven habits of highly effective people: Restoring the character ethic.* New York, NY: Fireside/Simon & Schuster. (Original work published 1989)

Da Costa, H. L., Jr. (2001). The Chamber of Reflection [online article]. *Grand Lodge of British Columbia and Yukon* [website]. (Originally presented 1999.) Consulted May 25, 2018 at http://freemasonry.bcy.ca/texts/gmd1999/pondering.html

Davie, G. (2002). *Europe: The exceptional case: Parameters of faith in the modern world.* London, England: Darton, Langman and Todd.

de Hoyos, A. (2018, July 14). Early Scots Masonry, the Royal Arch, and the Scottish Rite. Presentation at symposium, "Masonry during the Age of Enlightenment," presented under the aegis of LegendsOfTheCraft.com; New York City, NY.

Florida Masonic Monitor (23rd ed., corrected). (1995). [Jacksonville, FL]: Grand Lodge of Florida.

Gentry, D. ([2016]). The Chamber of Reflection and Freemasonry [online article]. *The Midnight Freemasons* [website]. Consulted May 25, 2018 at http://www.midnightfreemasons.org/2016/11/the-chamber-of-reflection-and.html

Gould, R. F. (2007). *The concise history of Freemasonry* (2nd ed., rev.). Mineola, NY: Dover. (Original work published 1920)

Grand Lodge of Florida. (1994). *Booklet no 1: The Lodge system of Masonic education* (rev. ed.). [Jacksonville, FL]: Author.

Grand Lodge of Free and Accepted Masons of the State of New York. (1958). *Monitor.* [New York, NY]: Author.

Grand Lodge of Maine, Ancient Free and Accepted Masons. (2013). *Maine Masonic mentoring handbook.* Holden, ME: Author. Consulted June 4, 2018 at https://www.mainemason.org/uploads/MaineMasonicMent oringHandbook.pdf

Grossman, L. (2016a, May 30). The geniuses who tracked down the gene [review of S. Mukherjee, *The Gene*]. *Time*, p. 56.

Grossman, L. (2016b, June 6). Video star: How YouTube celebrity PewDiePie reinvented fame. *Time*, pp. 52-56.

Halleran, M. A. (2010). *The better angels of our nature: Freemasonry in the American Civil War.* Tuscaloosa, AL: The University of Alabama Press.

Hammer, A. (2010). *Observing the Craft: The pursuit of excellence in Masonic labour and observance.* N.p.: Mindhive Books.

Hammer, A. (2012). To await a time with patience: Explaining the Chamber of Reflection [online article]. Consulted May 25, 2018 at http://www.masonicrestorationfoundation.org/documents/ A%20Time%20With%20Patience.pdf

Henderson, K. (2001). The European system of Freemasonry: A prescription for Masonic renewal [online document]. *Masonic Dictionary* [website]. Consulted May 26, 2018 at http://www.masonicdictionary.com/european.html

Hodapp, C. (2016, February 10). London Masons donating £2 million for air ambulance [blog post]. *Freemasons for Dummies* [blog]. Consulted June 14, 2016 at http://freemasonsfordummies.blogspot.com/2016/02/londo n-masons-donating-2-million-for.html

Holmes, D. L. (2006). *The faiths of the founding fathers.* New York, NY: Oxford University Press.

Hudson, P. A. (2007). Grand oration. In *Proceedings of the One Hundred and Seventy-Eighth Annual Communication of the M:.W:. Grand Lodge F.& A.M. of Florida, held at Orlando, Florida, May 28, 29, and 30* (pp. 272-275). [Jacksonville, FL]: The M:.W:. Grand Lodge of Free and Accepted Masons of Florida.

Jacob, M. C. (2010). *The scientific revolution: A brief history with documents*. Boston, MA: Bedford/St. Martin's.

Jones, B. (2011). Chamber of Reflection – Religious Studies final project [online video]. *Brad Jones* [YouTube online video channel]. Consulted May 25, 2018 at https://www.youtube.com/watch?v=frEVXfkJR90

Kinnaman, D., with A. Hawkins (2011). *You lost me: Why young Christians are leaving church ... and rethinking faith*. Grand Rapids, MI: Baker Publishing Group.

Knights of the North [C. L. Hodapp, ed.]. (2006). *Laudable pursuit: A 21st century response to Dwight Smith*. N.p.: Authors.

Koltko-Rivera, M. E. (2007, August). How should Masons respond to anti-Masonry? *The Philalethes: The Journal of Masonic Research and Letters, 60*(4), pp. 77, 87.

Koltko-Rivera, M. E. (2011). *Freemasonry: An introduction*. New York, NY: Tarcher/Penguin.

Koltko-Rivera, M. E. (Summer, 2016). Why write the lodge history? *Empire State Mason Magazine, 65*(2), p. 35. Online at http://www.masonichomeny.org/assets/ESM/Mason-2016-Sum-Final2.pdf#page=35

Koltko-Rivera, M. E. (2017). *The mysteries of Freemasonry: Essays on Masonic history, symbolism, the esoteric, and the future of*

Freemasonry. Weehawken, NJ: The School of Freemasonry Books.

Koltko-Rivera, M. E. (2018, August 7). *5 problems causing the Masonic membership crisis (Part 2 of series)* [online video]. *The Resurgence of Freemasonry* [YouTube channel], at https://youtu.be/ehs2uouVLqY

Lightfoot, J. P. (1934). *Lightfoot's Manual of the Lodge, or Monitorial instructions in the three degrees of Symbolic Masonry*. [Waco, TX]: Grand Lodge of Texas, A.F. & A.M.

Livingstone. (2014). The Chamber of Reflection [online article]. *Masonology: All things Freemason, since 6013 A.L.* [website]. Consulted May 25, 2018 at https://masonologyblog.wordpress.com/2014/01/07/the-chamber-of-reflection/

Livingstone. (2015). Can Masonry save God? [online article]. *Masonology: All things Freemason, since 6013 A.L.* [website]. Consulted May 25, 2018 at https://masonologyblog.wordpress.com/author/masonologylivingstone/

Lomas, R. (2003). *Freemasonry and the birth of modern science*. Gloucester, MA: Fair Winds Press.

Lombardo, G. (2006). The Chamber of Reflection [online article]. *ESNET: Selected Esotericism Readings*. (Republished from *Lodge Room International Magazine*, June 2006 issue.) Consulted May 25, 2018 at http://www.esonet.com/News-file-article-sid-406.html

"London Freemasons pledge £2million for 2nd helicopter" [online news article]. (2015, March 5). *Support London's Air Ambulance* [website]. Consulted June 14, 2016 at http://londonsairambulance.co.uk/our-service/news/2015/03/london-freemasons-pledge-2million-for-second-helicopter

Martinez, C. A. M., Jr. (2009). The anteroom or Chamber of Reflection: An omitted indispensable part of our ritual [online article]. *Freemason Information.* Consulted May 25, 2018, at http://freemasoninformation.com/2009/06/the-anteroom-or-chamber-of-reflection/

Masonic Lodge of Education [website]. (2018). Consulted June 4, 2018 at https://www.masonic-lodge-of-education.com/

Masonic Service Association of North America [MSANA]. (2005). *It's about time! Moving Masonry into the 21ˢᵗ century.* Silver Spring, MD: Masonic Information Center. Online at https://www.msana.com/downloads/abouttime.pdf and at http://www.msana.com/abouttime_foreward.asp .

Masonic Service Association of North America [MSANA]. (n.d. [ca. 2017]). *Masonic membership statistics 2015-2016: Membership totals since 1924* [online document]. Consulted May 21, 2018 at http://www.msana.com/msastats.asp

The Most Worshipful Grand Lodge of Free and Accepted Masons of Florida. (2008). *Mentor's manual.* [Jacksonville, FL]: Author. Consulted June 4, 2018 at http://grandlodgefl.com/docs/GLF_Publications/GL217%20Mentors%20Manual.pdf

The Most Worshipful Grand Lodge of Free and Accepted Masons of Florida. (2018). *Grand Lodge of Florida: Masonic Education: General Publications* [web page]. Consulted June 4, 2018 at http://grandlodgefl.com/glf_publications.html

The Right Worshipful Grand Lodge of Free and Accepted Masons of Pennsylvania. (2010). *The mentor program.* [Philadelphia, PA]: Author. Consulted June 4, 2018 at

http://www.50thdistrict.com/Mentor%20Program/TheMent
orProgram.pdf

Prothero, S. (2008). *Religious literacy: What every American needs to know—and doesn't*. New York, NY: HarperOne. (Original work published 2007)

Ridley, J. (2001). *The Freemasons: A history of the world's most powerful secret society*. New York, NY: Arcade Publishing. (Original work published 1999)

Singer, H. T., & Lang, O. (1981). *New York Freemasonry: A bicentennial history, 1781-1981*. [New York, NY]: The Grand Lodge of Free and Accepted Masons of the State of New York.

Smoley, R. (1997, Summer). Masonic civilization. *Gnosis*, no. 44, pp. 12-16. Available online at http://www.gnosismagazine.com/intros/intro44.html . (This essay is reprinted, with some revisions, in Smoley, 2013.)

Smoley, R. (2013). *Supernatural: Writings on an unknown history*. New York, NY: Tarcher/Penguin.

Stavish, M. (2002). The Chamber of Reflection [online paper]. Consulted May 25, 2018 at http://www.themasonictrowel.com/ebooks/fm_freemasonr y/Stavish_-_The_Chamber_of_Reflection.pdf

Sternberg, R. J. (2003). *Wisdom, intelligence, and creativity synthesized*. New York, NY: Cambridge University Press.

Stewart, G. (2016). Chamber of Reflection – Symbols and symbolism [online video]. *Masonic Traveler* [YouTube online video channel]. Consulted May 25, 2018 at https://www.youtube.com/watch?v=9Uc_pvZZf74

Tresner, J. T., II (2016, March/April). The long road [in part, a review of D. J. West, *Managing Freemasonry: A book of optimism*]. *The Scottish Rite Journal*, pg. 27.

Twenge, J. M., Sherman, R. A., Exline, J. J., & Grubs, J. B. (2016, January-March). Declines in American adults' religious participation and beliefs, 1972-2014. *SAGE Open*, pp. 1-13. DOI: 10.1177/2158244016638133 . Online at http://sgo.sagepub.com/content/6/1/2158244016638133

United States Census Bureau, Population Division. (2000). *Historical national population estimates: July 1, 1900 to July 1, 1999* [rev. ed.; online document]. Consulted May 21, 2018 at https://www2.census.gov/programs-surveys/popest/tables/1900-1980/national/totals/popclockest.txt

United States Census Bureau, Population Division. (2002). *Time series of intercensal state population estimates: April 1, 1990 to April 1, 2000* [online document]. Consulted May 21, 2018 at https://www.census.gov/data/tables/time-series/demo/popest/intercensal-1990-2000-state-and-county-totals.html

United States Census Bureau, Population Division. (2011). *Intercensal estimates of the resident population by sex and age for the United States: April 1, 2000 to July 1, 2010* [online document]. (n.d.). Consulted May 21, 2018 at https://www.census.gov/data/tables/time-series/demo/popest/intercensal-2000-2010-national.html

United States Census Bureau, Population Division. (2017). *Monthly population estimates for the United States: April 1, 2010 to December 1, 2018* [online document]. Consulted May 21, 2018 at

https://www.census.gov/data/tables/2017/demo/popest/nati
on-total.html#par_textimage_2011805803

United States Census Bureau. (2018a, March 13). *Projected
population by single year of age, sex, race, and Hispanic origin
for the United States: 2016-2060* [online document]. (n.d.).
Consulted May 21, 2018 at
https://www.census.gov/data/datasets/2017/demo/popproj/
2017-popproj.html

United States Census Bureau. (2018b, May 21, 20:05 UTC). *U.S.
and world population clock* [online streaming website]. Online
at www.census.gov/popclock/

United States Department of Health, Education, and Welfare,
Public Health Service. (1959). *Vital statistics of the United
States: 1959, Volume 1.* Washington, DC: U. S. Government
Printing Office. (.pdf document online at
http://www.cdc.gov/nchs/data/vsus/VSUS_1959_1.pdf)

Williamson, J. M. (2016, Fall). The Grand Master's address to
the brethren. *The Empire State Mason, 65*(3), pp. 2, 4-8.
Online at http://www.masonichomeny.org/assets/Mason-
Fall-Final.pdf .

Index

About the Author

Mark Koltko-Rivera was raised a Mason in Winter Park Masonic Lodge #239, in Florida. He belongs to Blue Lodges, Scottish Rite, York Rite, and invitational bodies in Florida and New York. He is the Past Grand Historian of the Grand Lodge of Free and Accepted Masons in the State of New York.

Bro. Koltko-Rivera has published Masonic scholarship in several publications: *The Philalethes* magazine; the *Transactions* of the American Lodge of Research (New York); *Further Light*, the transactions of the Florida Lodge of Research; and *Heredom: The Transactions of the Scottish Rite Research Society*, as well as in *The Plumbline*, published by the same organization.

Brother Koltko-Rivera is the author of two previous books on Freemasonry: *Freemasonry: An Introduction* (Tarcher/Penguin, 2011) and *The Mysteries of Freemasonry* (2017), the latter being a collection of his Masonic essays.

He holds a doctoral degree from the Department of Applied Psychology at New York University (NYU). He is an elected Fellow of the American Psychological Association. For his scholarship, he has received several awards: the Margaret Gorman Early Career Award in the psychology of religion (from the Society for the Psychology of Religion and Spirituality), the Carmi Harari Early Career Award for Inquiry (Society for Humanistic Psychology), and, on two occasions, the George A. Miller Award for an outstanding recent article on general psychology (Society for General Psychology). He has taught at NYU, the University of Central Florida, Hunter College of the City University of New York, and elsewhere.

He was born and raised on the Lower East Side of Manhattan in New York City, where he long lived in the East Village. He graduated from Regis High School (NYC), and holds an undergraduate degree from Haverford College and a master's degree from Fordham University.

Dr. Koltko-Rivera has four grown children and a lively group of grandchildren.

His website is listed at the conclusion of the Preface to this book; he may be reached through the Contact page there.

Bro. Mark Koltko-Rivera's
Online Masonic Community

- Facebook page: "The Resurgence of Freemasonry"

- Facebook page: "The Freemason Mark"

- Facebook page: "Masonic Writings of Mark Koltko-Rivera"

- Facebook group: "Masonic Education Beyond the Lodge Room"

- YouTube Channel: "Resurgence of Freemasonry," online at: https://bit.ly/2LN7whz

---

Forthcoming in Fall 2018

Masonic Education:
A Guide for Instructors and Speakers

Bro. Koltko-Rivera's Masonic books will be announced to his online Masonic community as soon as they are available. "Follow" one or more of his Facebook pages, join the Facebook group "The Resurgence of Freemasonry," or subscribe to his YouTube channel to be informed of his future publications.